The Metropolitan Opera Presents

Wolfgang Amadeus Mozart's

Così fan tutte

The Metropolitan Opera Presents

Wolfgang Amadeus Mozart's

Così fan tutte

Music by Wolfgang Amadeus Mozart

Libretto by Lorenzo Da Ponte

AMADEUS PRESS
An Imprint of Hal Leonard Corporation

The **Met** ropolitan **Opera**

Published in 2014 by Amadeus Press
An Imprint of Hal Leonard Corporation
7777 West Bluemound Road
Milwaukee, WI 53213

Trade Book Division Editorial Offices
33 Plymouth St., Montclair, NJ 07042

English translation of libretto copyright © 1997 by Leyerle Publications, 28 Stanley Street, Mt. Morris, New York 14510. English translation by Nico Castel. Originally published by Leyerle Publications as part of *The Libretti of Mozart's Complete Operas*, in two volumes. These publications, and others in the Leyerle Opera Libretti series, are available directly from Leyerle's website at www.leyerlepublications.com.

Printed in the United States of America

Book design by Mark Lerner

Library of Congress Cataloging-in-Publication Data is available upon request.

ISBN 978-1-57467-445-3

www.amadeuspress.com

CONTENTS

Florence Easton as Fiordiligi, 1922
HERMAN MISHKIN/METROPOLITAN OPERA ARCHIVES

INTRODUCTION

Among Mozart's major operas, *Così fan tutte* was the last to find a permanent place in the repertoire. For 100 years after its composer's death, it was mostly performed in adaptations and under different titles, since its story of romantic deception was seen as immoral at the time. Not until the end of the 19th century did this masterpiece return to the stage in its original form.

The Met first presented *Così* in 1922, in a production designed by the great Joseph Urban that marked the opera's US premiere, and the opera finally established itself in the repertoire for good nearly 30 years later with a legendary 1951 staging directed by Alfred Lunt. In more recent decades, Met Music Director James Levine has championed *Così*, making sure it returns to the repertoire regularly. Despite its relatively short history with our company, *Così fan tutte* has attracted some of the greatest Met singers, who have made memorable appearances in it—including Lucrezia Bori, Eleanor Steber, Kiri Te Kanawa, Tatiana Troyanos, Cecilia Bartoli, Richard Tucker, Håkan Hagegård, and Thomas Hampson, among others.

All of these extraordinary artists, and many others, are pictured in the archival photos you will find in this book. As part of our new series, *The Metropolitan Opera Presents*, this volume also includes the full libretto of *Così fan tutte* in Italian and English, a synopsis, a program note with historical background information, and the "In Focus" feature we provide in the Met's house program every night—a brief summary of key aspects of the opera. The books in this series are designed to give readers an in-depth introduction to some of the greatest works in the operatic repertoire (previous volumes are dedicated to *Tosca* and *La Bohème*). Whether you experience *Così fan tutte* at the Met, on the radio, online, or as part of our *Live in HD* movie-theater transmissions, I hope that on these pages you will find all you need to know to fully enjoy and appreciate this masterful and unique piece of music theater.

Peter Gelb
General Manager
Metropolitan Opera

To learn more about Met productions, Live in HD *movie-theater transmissions, Met membership, and more, visit metopera.org.*

The Metropolitan Opera Presents

Wolfgang Amadeus Mozart's

Così fan tutte

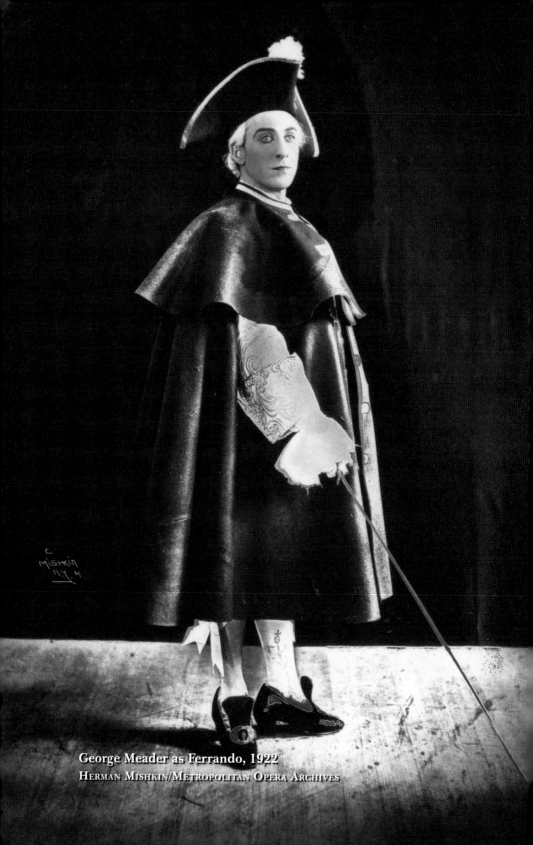

George Meader as Ferrando, 1922
HERMAN MISHKIN/METROPOLITAN OPERA ARCHIVES

Synopsis

Act I

Naples, late 18th century. Two young officers, Ferrando and Guglielmo, boast about the beauty and virtue of their girls, the sisters Fiordiligi and Dorabella. Their older friend, the cynical Don Alfonso, declares that a woman's constancy is like the phoenix—everyone talks about it but no one has ever seen it. He proposes a wager of one hundred sequins: if they'll give him one day and do everything he asks, he will prove to them that the sisters are unfaithful, like all other women. Amused, the young men agree.

Fiordiligi and Dorabella think of their lovers, imagining that they will soon be married. Alfonso's plot begins when he arrives with terrible news: the young officers have been called away to their regiment. Ferrando and Guglielmo appear, apparently heartbroken, and the four make tearful farewells. As the soldiers leave, the two women and Alfonso wish them a safe journey.

The sisters' maid, Despina, complains about how much work she has to do around the house. The girls enter and Dorabella vents her despair. Despina refuses to take them seriously: they should simply find new lovers, since men are unworthy of a woman's fidelity. Fiordiligi and Dorabella are shocked. Alfonso arrives and bribes Despina to assist him, without revealing his plot. Ferrando and Guglielmo enter, disguised as "Albanians," and declare their admiration for the ladies, each addressing the other's girlfriend.

The sisters firmly reject their advances, Fiordiligi comparing her constancy to a rock in a storm. The men are confident of winning the bet. Ferrando expresses his love for Dorabella, and the two friends leave.

As the sisters continue to lament the absence of their lovers, the "foreigners" return, pretending to have poisoned themselves in despair over their rejection. Despina and Alfonso go off to fetch help, leaving the two girls to care for the strangers, who find the situation highly amusing. Despina reappears disguised as a doctor and pretends to draw out the poison with a magnet. When Ferrando and Guglielmo request kisses in order to fully recover, the sisters again reject them, but it is clear they're beginning to show interest in the strangers.

Act II

Despina lectures her mistresses on how to handle men, and the sisters agree that there can be no harm in a little flirtation. They decide on their partners, each picking the other's suitor. Guglielmo, flirting with Dorabella, succeeds in replacing her portrait of Ferrando with his own gift. Ferrando has less luck with Fiordiligi, but when he has left, she struggles with her emotions.

Ferrando is certain that they have won the wager. Guglielmo is happy to hear that Fiordiligi has been faithful to him, but when he shows his friend the portrait he took from Dorabella, Ferrando is furious. Guglielmo, adopting Alfonso's philosophy, blames it on the women. He asks Alfonso to pay him his half of the winnings, but Alfonso reminds him that the day is not yet over.

Fiordiligi reproaches her sister for her behavior, but Dorabella replies that love is a thief who rewards those who obey him. Alone, Fiordiligi decides to join Guglielmo at the front, when suddenly Ferrando appears. He tries one last time to seduce her and succeeds.

Guglielmo is furious, but Alfonso again declares that this is the way women are. A man who has been deceived can blame only himself.

The sisters have agreed to marry the "foreigners." Everything is ready and Alfonso arrives with the notary—Despina in another disguise. As Fiordiligi and Dorabella sign the contract, military music announces the return of their former lovers. In a panic, they hide their intended husbands, who return as their real selves, first pretending surprise at their reception, then, when they discover the marriage contract, blaming the girls and threatening revenge. Finally, the men reveal their disguised identities, and Fiordiligi and Dorabella ask forgiveness. Alfonso bids the lovers learn their lesson.

Lucrezia Bori as Despina, 1922
HERMAN MISHKIN/METROPOLITAN OPERA ARCHIVES

In Focus

William Berger

Premiere: Vienna, Burgtheater, 1790

The third and final collaboration between Mozart and librettist Lorenzo Da Ponte is a fascinating paradox: a frothy comedy of manners with an intensely dark take on human nature; an old story (it has antecedents in Boccaccio, Shakespeare, and Cervantes, among others) with a startlingly modern tone; and a beautiful score depicting questionable behavior. The premise is simple: two friends brag that their fiancées, who happen to be sisters, are incapable of infidelity. An older, more philosophical man bets that he can prove them wrong in 24 hours and enlists the help of the sisters' devious maid to help him in his practical joke. He coerces each young man to seduce the other's fiancée, which they do successfully. Although the bet is lost, the philosopher advises his friends to forgive their fiancées and to learn from the experience—after all, "all women act like that" (to paraphrase the opera's title, which is famously difficult to translate).

The Setting

The opera is set in Naples. With its natural beauty and abundant sunshine, the city became the equivalent of a tourist destination in the 18th century. It has been suggested that the preponderance of woodwinds in the score is meant to evoke the breezy atmosphere of the seashore.

The Creators

Wolfgang Amadeus Mozart (1756–1791) was the son of a Salzburg court musician and composer, Leopold, who was also his principal teacher and exhibited him as a musical prodigy throughout Europe. His works continue to enthrall audiences around the world, and his achievements in opera, in terms of beauty, vocal challenge, and dramatic insight, remain unsurpassed. The extraordinary Lorenzo Da Ponte (1749–1838) led an adventurous life in Venice and Vienna. He converted from Judaism as a youth and joined the Catholic Church, where he took Holy Orders. He supplied librettos for the prominent composers of his time, including Antonio Salieri, and collaborated with Mozart on *Così fan tutte*, *Le Nozze di Figaro*, and *Don Giovanni*. Da Ponte migrated to America and eventually settled in New York, where he was granted the first chair of Italian at Columbia College (now University), and where he was instrumental in developing an audience for Italian opera.

The Music

The score of *Così* is elegant and refined on its surface and dramatically insightful on closer inspection. The Act I trio "Soave sia il vento" ("Let the breeze be gentle"), for example, is widely recognized as one of Mozart's most ravishing creations, but the contrary shape of Don Alfonso's and the two women's vocal lines clearly depicts divergent thoughts. In fact, it is often possible in this opera to tell who is siding with whom, and to what degree, in the various ensembles. The characters' development is apparent in the diversity of their solos: there is melodic simplicity in Guglielmo's Act I aria, in which he describes his own physical charms. Dorabella's self-pity in her Act I aria, "Smanie implacabili" ("Implacable torments"), is followed in the second act by the remarkably cheerful

"È Amore un ladroncello" ("Love is a little thief"), as she adapts to the new situation. Fiordiligi's progress is even more extreme: her Act I solo, "Come scoglio" ("Like a rock"), is highly dramatic, with leaps, drops, and runs up and down a two-octave range. It is both a supreme example of the show-stopping arias of 18th-century opera, and—in the context of the piece—a parody of the form. Unlike the more frivolous Dorabella, Fiordiligi demonstrates genuine human pathos, especially in her extended Act II lament, "Per pietà" ("Have pity"). Conversely, the maid Despina's arias are intensely word-driven and less about noble melody, while the lack of extended solos for Don Alfonso is appropriate to the enigma of his motivations and personality.

Così fan tutte at the Met

The Met gave the opera's US premiere in 1922, in a production designed by Joseph Urban and conducted by Artur Bodanzky, with a cast including Florence Easton, Lucrezia Bori, and Giuseppe De Luca. An English-language production directed by Alfred Lunt was unveiled in 1951, starring Eleanor Steber, Blanche Thebom, Patrice Munsel, Richard Tucker, Frank Guarrera, and John Brownlee. Among those who appeared in this production over the following years were Teresa Stich-Randall (1961–62) and Leontyne Price (1965) as Fiordiligi and Roberta Peters as Despina (28 performances from 1953 to 1965, and an additional two in 1975 to mark her 25th anniversary with the Met). This same production later moved to the new Met at Lincoln Center, where it was given in Italian with artists such as Teresa Stratas as Despina and Walter Berry as Don Alfonso (in 1971–72). A new production by Colin Graham appeared in 1982 with James Levine conducting Kiri Te Kanawa, Maria Ewing, Kathleen Battle, David Rendall, James Morris (as Guglielmo), and Donald Gramm. Revivals featured Pilar Lorengar, Ann Murray, Tatiana Troyanos, Hei-Kyung Hong, Håkan Hagegård, Thomas Hampson, and Cornell MacNeil. The current production opened in 1996, with James Levine conducting and Carol Vaness, Susanne Mentzer, Jerry Hadley, Dwayne Croft, Thomas Allen, and Cecilia Bartoli in her Met debut as Despina. Other notable appearances in this production have included Renée Fleming, Miah Persson, Susanna Phillips, Dawn Upshaw, Danielle de Niese, Susan Graham, Magdalena Kožená, Isabel Leonard, Paul Groves, Matthew Polenzani, and Nathan Gunn.

Frances Peralta as Dorabella and Florence Easton as Fiordiligi, 1922

Richard Tucker as Ferrando with director Alfred Lunt, 1951
SEDGE LEBLANG/METROPOLITAN OPERA ARCHIVES

Program Note

Cori Ellison

Dramma giocoso—"jocular drama"—sounds like "hot ice" or "cruel kindness." This oxymoronic term, coined by the 18th-century Venetian playwright Carlo Goldoni, is often applied to *Le Nozze di Figaro*, *Don Giovanni*, and *Così fan tutte*, the trio of operatic masterpieces on which Wolfgang Amadeus Mozart collaborated with librettist Lorenzo Da Ponte. And perhaps no opera is more deserving of the designation than *Così*, a work as ambiguous as its title is untranslatable (let's call it "All Women Act Like That" or, more literally, "So Do They All"). During the last 100 years alone, critics have variously described it as "a glorious soap-bubble," "a deep and unsettling masterpiece," "a musical lark," and "a profound and terrifying tragicomedy"; they have praised both its "enchanted artificiality" and its "acute realism."

So what is *Così fan tutte*—a proto-Freudian nightmare or a sort of Enlightenment *I Love Lucy*? The answer, of course, lies somewhere in between. Despite its easy laughs, its apparent neat symmetries, and the tidy paean to reason with which it ends, *Così* is a web of ambiguities that will surely send you home whistling the tunes but also, perhaps, reaching for the Maalox.

Così fan tutte claims paradox as its birthright. Though it is a *dernier cri* of the Enlightenment, during its gestation in 1789 the Bastille was falling and with it the clear, prosaic equilibrium of the Age of Reason. And *Così*—populated by a pair of prideful men who place a wager on their fiancées' fidelity, a pair of fiancées who fail their test, a worldly wise philosopher who manipulates the action, and a cheeky serving maid who aids him—flew in the face of all that was dear to incipient Romanticism.

As a result *Così* has suffered a checkered performance history. The opera as we know it all but disappeared during the 19th century. It was seen only in bowdlerizations and wholesale rearrangements designed to preserve its "heavenly melodies" while mitigating its vexing plot. The earliest known hatchet job, C. F. Bretzner's *Die Wette, oder Mädchenlist und Liebe*, presented in Hamburg in 1796, has Despina revealing the men's plot before the "Albanians" arrive, so that the sisters appear less foolish. At the end, the men abjectly beg the ladies' pardon, and a real notary is on hand to marry the couples. *Die Zauberprobe, oder So Sind Sie Alle*, devised by G. F. Treitschke in Vienna in 1814, renders Don Alfonso a sorcerer and Despina a sprite, which not only satisfied the public's appetite for magic but also absolved the lovers of any moral responsibility for their actions. In Krebel's *Mädchen Sind Mädchen* (Stuttgart, 1816), the men put their sweethearts to the test after returning from a lengthy journey. In C. A. Herclots's *Die Verfängliche Wette* (Berlin, 1822), the women are tested not by Ferrando and Guglielmo but by friends of theirs, and in Bernhard Gugler's *So Sind Sie Treu?* (Stuttgart, 1858), each man tests his own fiancée. It was not until 1896, in Munich, that *Così* was again seen more or less in its original form. (The Metropolitan Opera didn't get around to producing *Così* at all until its American premiere in 1922, 39 years after the Met first presented *Don Giovanni* and 28 years after *Le Nozze di Figaro*.)

Each of the mutilations of *Così* documented above points to one of its "problems." First of all, the Romantics, drawn onward by Goethe's *Ewig-Weibliche*, were scandalized by the opera's supposedly unflattering portrayal of women. Little more than a year after *Così*'s premiere at Vienna's Burgtheater on January 26, 1790, the actor Friedrich Ludwig Schroeder recorded in his diary that the opera was "a miserable thing, which lowers all women, cannot possibly please female spectators, and will therefore not make its fortune." (He cannot have listened too carefully to Fiordiligi's noble Act II aria and her duet with Ferrando, both steeped in depth and humanity.) Though the loaded issue of sexual fidelity is as central to *Figaro* and *Giovanni* as it is to *Così*, the former works didn't upset people as profoundly, perhaps because in those operas the transgressors are men and, anyway, they get their lumps at the end.

Vying with the public's distaste for *Così*'s apparent wantonness was disdain for its seeming implausibility. In 1863, Viennese critic Eduard Hanslick fulminated over "the continuing blindness of the two heroines, who do not recognize their fiancés only a quarter hour after they have been caressing them, and who stupidly take their chambermaid to be first a doctor and then a notary just because she is wearing a wig." Never mind that the element of disguise also figures prominently in both *Figaro* and *Giovanni* (not to mention *Fidelio*).

Così's detractors have also objected to its allegedly unrealistic time span: how could the fickle heroines change their affections in a mere day? Here, it's vital to remember that a devoted Classicist like Da Ponte would never have failed to observe the Aristotelian unities of time, place, and action, and that these unities were often meant to be taken as symbolic.

The paradox of *Così* extends to its provenance. Purportedly based on nothing more distinguished than a snippet of contemporary Viennese gossip, it lacks a literary pedigree like that of *Figaro* (Beaumarchais) or *Giovanni* (Tirso de Molina). At the same time, *Così*'s plot may boast true mythological status, tracing its heritage back to the story of Cephalus, whose fidelity is tested by his disguised wife Procris in Ovid's *Metamorphoses*, and on, in varied forms, through Terence, Plautus, Ariosto, Boccaccio, Cervantes, and perhaps most notably, Shakespeare's *A Midsummer Night's Dream*.

Yet it also owes much, as do all *opere buffe*, to the back-alley antics of *commedia dell'arte*.

This gave Mozart license to go to town with one of the pet conceits of his later operas: constantly colliding the parallel universes of *opera seria* and *opera buffa*. The characters in *Così*, ostensibly a comic opera, frequently lapse into seria-speak, sometimes offered up in parody (Dorabella's "Smanie implacabili," Fiordiligi's "Come scoglio"), sometimes in a spirit of deep sincerity (Fiordiligi's "Per pietà," all three of Ferrando's arias, and their majestic duet). But Mozart and Da Ponte never let us wallow there too long, and they particularly enjoy pulling the rug from under us by reminding us that we are in the theater. The sublime "Soave sia il vento" trio of Act I has barely faded away when Don Alfonso congratulates himself on his acting; at the end of Act I, the sisters fulminate at their would-be suitors while the others tell us how amusing a "scene" it is. And a bit earlier in the same finale, the cast crystallizes *Così*'s duality for us: the sisters deem the situation a "tragedy," while the men call it a "farce." These are but a few of the things that give *Così* its sweet-and-sour flavor.

Those distressed by *Così* have sometimes consoled themselves with the notion that their beloved Mozart had been forced to write it against his will. This fiction was launched in 1798 and perpetuated by his first biographer, Franz Xaver Niemetschek, and supported by Mozart's brother-in-law, the artist Joseph Lange, who in 1808 held that "everywhere people wonder how that great mind could lower itself to waste its heavenly melodies on so feeble a concoction of text. It was not in his power to refuse the commission, and the text was expressly served on him."

True, an imperial commission was not to be turned down; the composition of *Così* was generated by Emperor Joseph II's enthusiasm for a successful Vienna revival of *Figaro*. And it is also true enough that the year 1789 found Mozart in straitened finances and that *Così* was hastily written in the space of four months, during which the composer sadly had little else to occupy his attention.

But in that brief span, Mozart lavished his finest inspiration on *Così*. For prodigal musical richness, for clear-eyed portrayal of the human condition, the world has never seen a more "glorious"—and "profound and unsettling"—"soap-bubble."

Eleanor Steber as Fiordiligi, 1951
METROPOLITAN OPERA ARCHIVES

COSÌ FAN TUTTE

(All Women Behave Like That)

ossia

(or)

LA SCUOLA DEGLI AMANTI

(The School for Lovers)

PERSONAGGI

Fiordiligi, dama ferrarese abitante in Napoli: soprano
Dorabella, dama ferrarese e sorella di Fiordiligi: mezzo-soprano
Ferrando, ufficiale, amante di Dorabella: tenore
Guglielmo, ufficiale, amante di Fiordiligi: baritono
Don Alfonso, vecchio filosofo: basso
Despina, cameriera: soprano

Soldati, servi e marinai

CHARACTERS

Fiordiligi, lady from Ferrara and sister to Dorabella, living in
  Naples: soprano

Dorabella, lady from Ferrara and sister to Fiordiligi, living in
  Naples: mezzo-soprano

Ferrando, lover of Dorabella, a soldier: tenor

Guglielmo, lover of Fiordiligi, a soldier: baritone

Don Alfonso, an old philosopher: bass

Despina, a maid: soprano

Soldiers, Sailors, Servants and Townspeople

ATTO PRIMO
ACT I

(Bottega di caffè. Ferrando, Guglielmo e Don Alfonso.)
(In a café a lively discussion is in progress between all three men.)

NO. 1 TERZETTO
NO. 1 TRIO

FERRANDO
La mia Dorabella capace non è: fedel quanto bella il cielo la fè!
My Dorabella able is not: faithful as lovely heaven made her!
(My Dorabella couldn't do that! Heaven made her as faithful as she is beautiful.)

GUGLIELMO
La mia Fiordiligi tradirmi non sa:
My Fiordiligi betray me cannot.

Uguale in lei credo costanza e beltà.
Equal in her I believe (is) constancy and beauty.
(I believe her loyalty equals her beauty.)

ALFONSO
Ho i crini già grigi, *ex cathedra*[1] parlo
I have the hairs already gray, from experience I speak,

(My hair is already gray, I speak from experience.)

ma tali litigi finiscano quà.
but such bickering let it be ended here.
(But let's stop this bickering right here and now.)

FERRANDO, GUGLIELMO
No, detto ci avete che infide esser ponno;[2]
No, told you have us that unfaithful be they can;
(No, you told us that they can be unfaithful;)

provar cel' dovete, se avete onestà.
prove it to us you must if you have honor.
(it's up to you to prove it to us, if you're a man of honor.)

ALFONSO
Tai prove lasciamo…
Such proofs let us forget about…

FERRANDO, GUGLIELMO
(metton mano alla spada)
(putting their hands on the hilts of their swords)
No, no, le vogliamo: o fuori la spada, rompiam l'amistà.
No, no, we want them, or out with the sword, let's break the
friendship.
(No, no, we want the proofs or else draw your sword and let's end
this friendship.)

ALFONSO
(a parte)
(aside)
O pazzo desire, cercar di scoprire
Oh insane desire, to try to discover

quel mal che, trovato, meschini ci fa.
that evil that, (once) found, miserable makes us.

FERRANDO, GUGLIELMO
Sul vivo mi tocca chi lascia di bocca sortire un accento
It cuts me to the quick, who allows from mouth come out a word

che torto le fa.
that injury does her.
(Anyone who dares say one word that may do her injury, cuts me
to the quick.)

GUGLIELMO
Fuor' la spada: scegliete qual di noi più vi piace.
Out the sword: choose which of us most you like.
(Out with your sword! And choose which one of us you like to
fight with.)

ALFONSO
Io son uomo di pace
I am a man of peace

e duelli non fo se non a mensa.
and duels I don't fight except at (the) dinner table.

FERRANDO
O battervi, o dir subito perché d'infedeltà
Either fight (with us), or tell us right now why of unfaithfulness

le nostre amanti sospettate capaci.
our sweethearts you suspect capable.
(Either fight with us or tell us immediately why you suspect our
sweethearts capable of being unfaithful.)

ALFONSO
Cara semplicità, quanto mi piaci!
Dear naiveté, how I like you!
(Dear innocence, how much I like you!)

FERRANDO
Cessate di scherzar, o giuro al cielo...
Stop joking, or I swear to heaven...

ALFONSO
Ed io, giuro alla terra, non scherzo, amici miei;
And I, I swear to earth, I'm not joking, friends mine;

solo saper vorrei, che razza dianimali son queste vostre belle,
only know I'd like what race of animals are these your beauties,
(I'd like to know what sort of animals your beauties might be,)

se han come tutti noi carne, ossa, e pelle,
if they have like all (of) us flesh, bones, and skin,

se mangian come noi, se veston gonne,
if they eat like us, if they wear skirts,

alfin, se Dee, se donne son...
finally, if goddesses, if women they are...
(and finally, whether they are goddesses or women...)

FERRANDO, GUGLIELMO
Son donne: ma, son tali...
They're women, but, they're such (women)...

ALFONSO
E in donne pretendete di trovar fedeltà?
And in women do you think to find fidelity?

Quanto mi piaci mai, semplicità!
How much I like you ever, naiveté!
(Dear innocence, how much I like you!)

NO. 2 TERZETTO
NO. 2 TRIO

ALFONSO
È la fede delle femmine come l'araba fenice,
Is the fidelity of women like the Arabian phoenix,[3]
(Fidelity in women is like the Arabian phoenix,)

che vi sia ciascun lo dice,
that it exists everyone says it,

dove sia…nessun lo sa.
where it is…nobody knows it.
(Everyone says it exists but no one knows where it is.)

FERRANDO
La fenice è Dorabella.
The phoenix is Dorabella.

GUGLIELMO
(con fuoco)
(with fire)
La fenice è Fiordiligi.
The phoenix is Fiordiligi.

ALFONSO
Non è questa, non è quella, non fu mai, non vi sarà.
It isn't this one, it isn't that one, it never was, it will never be.
(It isn't one or the other, it never existed, it will never exist.)

È la fede delle femmine come l'araba, etc.

FERRANDO, GUGLIELMO
La fenice è Dorabella, etc.

ALFONSO
Nessun lo sa.

FERRANDO
Scioccherie di poeti!
Nonsense of poets!

GUGLIELMO
Scempiaggini di vecchi.
Foolishnesses of old men!
(Oh what senile foolishness!)

ALFONSO
Or bene; udite, ma senza andar in collera:
Now then; listen, but without going into (a) fury:

qual prova avete voi che ognor costanti
What proof have you that always faithful

vi sien le vostre amanti?
may be your sweethearts?
(What proof do you have that your sweethearts may be always faithful?)

Chi vi fè sicurtà che invariabili sono i lor cori?
Who gave you assurance that immutable are their hearts?
(How can you be so sure that their hearts aren't fickle?)

FERRANDO
Lunga esperienza...
Long experience...
(We've known them for so long...)

GUGLIELMO
Nobil educazion...
Noble upbringing...
(They're so well brought up...)

FERRANDO
Pensar sublime...
Thinking sublime...
(Their sublimity of thoughts...)

GUGLIELMO
Analogia d'umor...
Compatibility of temperament...

FERRANDO
Disinteresse...
Unselfishness...

GUGLIELMO
Immutabil caratter...
Steadfast character...

FERRANDO
Promesse...
Promises...
(The promises they've made...)

GUGLIELMO
Proteste…
Protestations (of love)…

FERRANDO
Giuramenti…
Oaths…

ALFONSO
Pianti, sospir, carezze, svenimenti. Lasciatemi un po' ridere…
Tears, sighs, caresses, swoonings. Allow me a bit to laugh…

FERRANDO
Cospetto, finite di deriderci!
Confound it, (will you) stop deriding us?
(Confound it! Will you stop making fun of us?)

ALFONSO
Pian piano: e se toccar con mano[4]
Take it easy: And if touch with hand

oggi vi fo che come l'altre sono?
today I make you that like all others they are?
(Take it easy: Supposing today I give you palpable proof that they
are like all other women?)

GUGLIELMO
Non si può dar!
That cannot be!

FERRANDO
Non è!
Not so!

ALFONSO
Giochiam!
Shall we wager!

FERRANDO
Giochiamo!
Let's wager!

ALFONSO
Cento zecchini.
A hundred sequins.[5]

GUGLIELMO
E mille se volete.
And a thousand if you like.

ALFONSO
Parola…
Word…
(Your word on it…)

FERRANDO
Parolissima.
Very much my word!

ALFONSO
E un cenno, un motto, un gesto,
And a sign, a word, a gesture,

giurate di non far di tutto questo alle vostre Penelopi.
swear to not give of all this to your Penelopes.[6]

FERRANDO
Giuriamo.
We swear.

ALFONSO
Da soldati d'onore?
As soldiers of honor?
(On your honor as soldiers?)

GUGLIELMO
Da soldati d'onore.
On our soldier's honor!

ALFONSO
E tutto quell farete ch'io vi dirò di far.
And all that you'll do that I tell you to do.
(And you'll do everything I tell you to do?)

FERRANDO
Tutto!
Everything!

GUGLIELMO
Tuttissimo!
Everything indeed!

ALFONSO
Bravissimi!
Good for you!

FERRANDO, GUGLIELMO
Bravissimo, signor Don Alfonsetto!
Excellent, *signor* Don Alfonsetto!

GUGLIELMO
A spese vostre or ci divertiremo.
At expense yours now we will enjoy ourselves.

(a Ferrando)
(to Ferrando)

E do cento zecchini[7] che faremo?
And with the hundred sequins what will we do?

NO. 3 TERZETTO
NO. 3 TRIO

FERRANDO
Una bella serenata far io voglio alla mia Dea.
A lovely serenade make I want to my goddess.
(I'd like to offer a serenade to my goddess.)

GUGLIELMO
In onor di Citerea un convito io voglio far.
In honor of Cythera[8] a banquet I want to give.

ALFONSO
Sarò anch'io dei convitati?
Will be also I among the invited ones?
(Will I also be invited?)

FERRANDO, GUGLIELMO
Ci sarete, sì Signor.
You will be, yes sir.

FERRANDO, GUGLIELMO, ALFONSO
E che brindis[9] replicati far vogliamo al dio d'amor!
And what toasts repeated offer we want to the god of love!
(And repeatedly we will offer toasts to the god of love!)

(Partono. Giardino sulla spiaggia del mare. Fiordiligi e Dorabella, che guardono ciascuna un medaglione.)

(They leave and the scene changes to a garden near the seashore where Fiordiligi and Dorabella are gazing at portraits inside lockets which hang from their necks.)

NO. 4 DUETTO
NO. 4 DUO

FIORDILIGI
Ah, guarda, sorella, se bocca più bella,
Ah, look, sister, if (a) mouth more lovely,

se aspetto più nobile si può ritrovar.
if (a) face more noble could be found.

DORABELLA
Osserva tu un poco che foco ha ne' sguardi,
Observe you a bit what fire he has in his gaze,

se fiamma, se dardi non sembran scoccar.
if flame, if darts doesn't it seem to shoot off.
(Look at the fire in his gaze, if it doesn't seem to fling flames and arrows!)

FIORDILIGI
Si vede un sembiante guerriero ed amante.
One sees a face of a warrior and a lover.

DORABELLA
Si vede una faccia che alletta e minaccia.
One sees a face that entices and menaces.

FIORDILIGI
Felice son io!
Happy am I!

DORABELLA
Io sono felice!
I am happy!

FIORDILIGI, DORABELLA
Se questo mio core mai cangia desio,
If this my heart ever changes desire,
(If my heart ever changes its affections,)

Amore mi faccia vivendo penar.
(May) love make me, living suffer.
(May the "god of love" make me suffer while still living.)
(May the "god of love" make me live in misery.)

FIORDILIGI
Mi par che stamattina volentieri farei la pazzarella:
I think that this morning gladly I'd play the little silly girl:
(I feel like doing something silly this morning:)

ho un certo foco, un certo pizzicor entro le vene…
I've a certain fire, a certain tingling inside my veins…

Quando Guglielmo viene, se sapessi che burla gli vo' far!
When Guglielmo comes, if you knew what joke on him I want to play!

DORABELLA
Per dirti il vero, qualche cosa di nuovo
To tell you the truth, some thing new

anch'io nell'alma provo: Io giurerei
also I in my soul I feel: I would swear

che lontano non siamo dagli imenei.[10]
that far we aren't from our weddings.

FIORDILIGI
Damni la mano: io voglio astrologarti:
Give me your hand, I want to tell your fortune.

Uh, che bell'*Emme*, e questo è un *pi*!
Oh, what lovely *M*, and this is a *P*!

Va bene: *m*atrimonio *p*resto.
All right: *m*atrimony *p*resently.

DORABELLA
Affe che ci avrei gusto!
By my faith that of it I'd have pleasure!
(I'd like that, by my faith!)

FIORDILIGI
Ed io non ci avrei rabbia.
And I not from it would have displeasure.
(And I wouldn't exactly be displeased by it!)

DORABELLA
Ma che diavol vuol dir che i nostri sposi
But what devil means that our lovers

ritardano a venir? Son già le sei…
are so late in coming? It's already six o'clock…
(But why the devil are our lovers so late in coming? It's already six o'clock…)

FIORDILIGI
Eccoli.
Here they are.

DORABELLA
Non son essi; è Don Alfonso, l'amico lor.
It isn't they. It's Don Alfonso, the friend theirs.

FIORDILIGI
Ben venga il Signor Don Alfonso!
Welcome, mister Don Alfonso!

ALFONSO
(entrando)
(entering)
Riverisco.
My respects.

DORABELLA
Cos'è, perché qui solo? Voi piangete, parlate per pietà,
What is it, why here alone? You are weeping, speak for pity's sake,

che cosa è nato? L'amante…
what has happened? My beloved…

FIORDILIGI
L'idol mio…
The idol mine…

NO. 5 ARIA

ALFONSO
Barbaro fato! Vorrei dir, e cor non ho:
Cruel fate! I'd like to tell you and heart I don't have:
(Oh cruel fate! I'd like to tell you but I don't have the heart.)

Balbettando il labbro va. Fuor la voce uscir non può,
Stammering the lip is. Out my voice come out cannot,
(My lips are stammering and my voice won't come out of my mouth,)

ma mi resta mezza qua.
but it sticks half here.
(and (my words) half stick here in my throat.)

Che farete, che farò? Oh, che gran fatalità!
What will you do, what will I do? Oh, what great disaster!

Dar di peggio non si può, ho di voi, di lor pietà.
Nothing worse could happen, I've for you, for them pity.

FIORDILIGI
Stelle, per carità, Signor Alfonso, non ci fate morir.
Stars, for pity's sake, Don Alfonso, don't make us die.
(Heavens! For pity's sake, Don Alfonso, don't make us die of suspense!)

ALFONSO
Convien armarvi, figlie mie, di costanza.
It is necessary to arm yourselves, daughters mine, with strength.
(My children, you must be strong.)

DORABELLA
O Dei, qual male è addivenuto mai,
Oh gods, what misfortune has occurred ever,
(Oh Gods! What misfortune has occurred,)

qual caso rio: forse è morto oil mio bene?
what thing evil: perhaps is dead my beloved?

FIORDILIGI
È mort il mio?
Is dead mine?
(Is my beloved dead?)

ALFONSO
Morti non son, ma poco men che morti.
Dead they aren't, but little less than dead.
(They aren't dead, but they might as well be.)

DORABELLA
Feriti?
Wounded?

ALFONSO
No.

FIORDILIGI
Ammalati?
Sick?

ALFONSO
Neppur.
Not even that.

FIORDILIGI
Che cosa dunque?
What then?

ALFONSO
Al marzial campo ordin regio li chiama.
To the battle field order royal calls them.
(A royal command summons them to battle.)

FIORDILIGI, DORABELLA
Ohimè, che sento!
Woe is me, what do I hear!

FIORDILIGI
E partiran?
And they will leave?
(And when will they leave?)

ALFONSO
Sul fatto.
Immediately.

DORABELLA
E none v'è modo d'impedirlo?
And isn't there (a) way to prevent it?

ALFONSO
Non v'è.
There isn't.

FIORDILIGI
Nè un solo addio…
Not even one single farewell…

ALFONSO
Gl'infelici non hanno coraggio di vedervi;
The poor hapless ones don't have the courage to see you;

ma se voi Io bramate, son pronti…
but if you wish it, they're ready…

DORABELLA
Dove son?
Where are they?

ALFONSO
Amici, entrate.
Friends, come in.

(Entrano Ferrando e Guglielmo in abito da viaggio.)
(Guglielmo and Ferrando enter, wearing travelling clothes.)

NO. 6 QUINTETTO
NO. 6 QUINTET

GUGLIELMO
Sento, o Dio, che questo piede è restio nel girle avante.
I feel, Oh God, that this foot is reluctant to step forward.

FERRANDO
Il mio labbro palpitante non può detto pronunziar.
My lips trembling cannot (one) word pronounce.

ALFONSO
Nei momenti più terribili sua virtù l'eroe palesa.
In the moments most terrible his mettle the hero reveals.
(The hero reveals his true mettle in the most terrible moments.)

FIORDILIGI, DORABELLA
Or che abbiam la nuova intesa,
Now that we have the news heard,

a voi resta a fare il meno;
to you remains to do the least;
(Now that we've heard the news, there remains one thing that you
can at least do for us;)

fate core, a entrambe in seno immergeteci l'acciar.
take heart, to both of us in (our) bosom plunge into us your steel.
(have courage and plunge your swords into our bosoms.)

FERRANDO, GUGLIELMO
Idol mio, la sorte incolpa se ti deggio abbandonar.
Idol mine, fate blame if I must you abandon.
(My beloved, fate is to blame for us having to leave you.)

DORABELLA
Ah no, no, non partirai.
Ah, no, no, you won't leave.

FIORDILIGI
No, crudel, non te ne andrai.
No, cruel one, you won't go from here.

DORABELLA
Voglio pria cavarmi il core.
I want first to tear out my heart.

FIORDILIGI
Pria ti vo' morire ai piedi.
First I want to die at your feet.

FERRANDO
(piano a Don Alfonso)
(aside, to Don Alfonso)
(Cosa dici?)
(What do you say?)

GUGLIELMO
(Te n'avvedi?)
(Do you see that?)

ALFONSO
(Saldo amico, finem lauda.)
(Steady, (my) friend, at the end praise.)

(Steady, my friends, save your praises for your women until the end.)

TUTTI
ALL
Il destin così defrauda le speranze de' mortali.
Destiny thus cheats the hopes of mortals.

Ah, chi mai fra tanti mali, chi mai può la vita amar?
Ah, who ever amid such grief can life love?
(Ah, who can love life amid so much grief?)

GUGLIELMO[11]
Non piangere, idol mio.
Don't weep, idol mine.

FERRANDO
Non disperanti, adorata mia sposa.
Do not despair, adored my bride.

ALFONSO
Lasciate lor tal sfogo:
Allow them that venting:
(Allow them to get it off their chests:)
(Let them have a good cry:)

è troppo giusta la cagion di quel pianto.
Is too just the reason for that weeping.
(They've got good reason to cry.)

FIORDILIGI
Chi sa s'io più ti veggio!
Who knows if ever again I will see you!

DORABELLA
Chi sa se più ritorni!
Who knows if ever again you will return!

(Si abbracciano teneramente.)
(The lovers embrace tenderly.)

FIORDILIGI
Lasciami questo ferro: ei mi dia morte
Leave me this sword: It will give me death

se mai barbara sorte in quel seno a me caro…
if ever barbarous fate in that bosom to me dear…
(if cruel fate should ever have my beloved's chest be pierced by a
sword in battle…)

DORABELLA
Morrei di duol, d'uopo non ho d'acciaro.[12]
I should die of grief, need I don't have for a sword.

FERRANDO, GUGLIELMO
Non farmi, anima mia, quest'infausti presagi;
Do not make my beloved, these dire predictions;

Proteggeran gli Dei la pace del tuo cor ne' giorni miei.
Will protect the gods the peace of your heart in the days mine.
(The gods will protect your peace of mind as long as I live.)

No. 7 DUETTO
No. 7 DUET

FERRANDO, GUGLIELMO
Al fato dàn legge quegli occhi vezzosi;
To our fate give law those eyes pretty;
(Those pretty eyes of yours decide our fate;)

amor li protegge, né i loro riposi
love protects them, nor their rest

le barbare stelle ardiscon turbar.
the cruel stars dare to disturb.
(love protects them and even the cruel stars won't dare disturb their rest.)

Il ciglio[13] sereno, mio bene, a me gira,
The eye serene, my beloved to me turn,
(Turn your peaceful eyes to me, my beloved,)

felice al tuo seno io spero tornar.
happy to your bosom I hope to return.

ALFONSO
(La commedia è graziosa e tutti due fan bella loro parte.)
(The comedy is charming and both play well their part.)

(Si sente un suono di tamburo.)
(A drum roll is heard.)

FERRANDO
O cielo, questo è il tamburo funesto,
Oh heaven, this is the drum fatal,

che a divider mi vien dal mio tesoro.
that to separate me comes from my treasure.
(Oh heavens! There is the fatal drum that comes to separate me from my beloved.)

ALFONSO
Ecco, amici, la barca.
There, friends, (is) the boat.

FIORDILIGI
Io manco.
I am fainting.

DORABELLA
Io moro.
I am dying.

NO. 8 CORO
NO. 8 CHORUS

Bella vita militar, ogni dì si cangia loco,
Lovely life military, every day one changes place,

oggi molto, doman poco, ora in terra ed or sul mar.
today a lot, tomorrow little, now on land, now at sea.

Il fragor di trombe e pifferi,
The blare of trumpets and fifes,

lo sparar di schioppi e bombe
the exploding of muskets and bombs

forza accresce al braccio
strength increases to arm

e all'anima vaga sol di trionfar.
and to the soul, longing only for triumph.
(gives strength to arms and soul longing for triumphs.)

ALFONSO
Non v'è più tempo, amici, andar conviene
There isn't any more time, friends, leave you must

ove il destino, anzi il dover v'invita.
where destiny, rather duty summons you.

FIORDILIGI
Mio cor...
My heart...

DORABELLA
Idolo mio...
Idol mine...

FERRANDO
Mio ben...
My beloved...

GUGLIELMO
Mia vita...
My life...

FIORDILIGI
Ah, per un sol momento...
Ah, for one sole moment...

ALFONSO
Del vostro reggimento già è partita la barca;
Of your regiment already has left the ship;
(Your regiment's ship has already left;)

Raggiungerla convien coi pochi amici
Catch up to it you must with the few friends

che su legno[14] piu lieve attendendo vi stanno.
who on (a) boat more light awaiting you.
(You must catch up to your ship on a smaller boat, on which a few
friends are awaiting you.)

FERRANDO, GUGLIELMO
Abbracciami, idol mio.
Embrace me, idol mine.

FIORDILIGI, DORABELLA
Muoio d'affanno.
I'm dying of grief.

NO. 9 QUINTETTO E CORO
NO. 9 QUINTET AND CHORUS

FIORDILIGI
(piangendo)
(in tears)
Di scrivermi ogni giorno giurami, vita mia!
To write me every day swear to me, life mine!
(Swear that you will write to me every day!)

DORABELLA
(piangendo)
(in tears)
Due volte ancora tu scrivimi se puoi.
Twice yet you write me if you can.

FERRANDO
Sii certa, o cara.
Be certain, oh dearest.

GUGLIELMO
Non dubitar, mio bene.
Don't doubt, my beloved.

ALFONSO
(a parte)
(aside)
(Io crepo se non rido!)
(I'll burst if I don't laugh!)

FIORDILIGI
Sii costante a me sol…
Be faithful to me alone…

DORABELLA
Serbati fido.
Keep yourself faithful (to me).

FERRANDO, GUGLIELMO, DORABELLA, FIORDILIGI
Addio. Mi si divide il cor, bell'idol mio!
Farewell. Is breaking in two my heart, lovely idol mine!

CORO
CHORUS

Bella vita militar, ecc.
Lovely life military, etc.

(Mentre si ripete il coro, Ferrando e Guglielmo entrano nella barca che poi s'allontana. I oldati partono, seguiti dagli uomini e dalle donne.)
(The young men leave and Dorabella and Fiordiligi are left alone with Alfonso.)

DORABELLA
(in atto di chi rinviene da un letargo)
(as if awaking from a trance)
Dove son?
Where are they?

ALFONSO
Son partiti.
They've left.

FIORDILIGI
Oh dipartenza crudelissima! amara!
Oh, departure most cruel (and) bitter!

ALFONSO
Fate core, carissime figliuole; guardate,
Take heart, dearest girls; look,

da lontano vi fan cenno con mano i cari sposi.
from afar they make you signs with their hand the dear lovers.
(your lovers are waving at you from far away.)

FIORDILIGI
(salutando)
(waving back)
Buon viaggio, mia vita!
Bon voyage, my life!

DORABELLA
(salutando)
(also waving)
Buon viaggio!
Bon voyage!

FIORDILIGI
Oh Dei, come veloce se ne va quella barca!
Oh gods how rapidly it is sailing that ship!

Già sparisce. Già non si vede più.
Already it's disappearing. Already it can't be seen any longer.

Deh, faccia il cielo ch'abbia prospero corso.
Ah, grant heaven that it may have (a) prosperous course.
(May heaven grant it a good voyage.)

DORABELLA
Faccia che al campo giunga con fortunati auspici.
Grant that at the battlefield it may arrive with fortunate prospects.
(May heaven grant that it arrive at the battlefield safe and sound.)

ALFONSO
E a voi salvi gli amanti, e a me gli amici.
And to you preserve your lovers, and to me the friends.
(And may heaven protect your lovers and my friends.)

NO. 10 TERZETTINO

FIORDILIGI, DORABELLA, ALFONSO
Soave sia il vento, tranquilla sia l'onda,
Gentle be the wind, tranquil be the wave,
(May the wind blow gently and the sea be calm,)

ed ogni elemento benigno risponda ai nostri desir.
and every element benign may answer to our desires.
(and may the elements be kind and grant our desires.)

(Fiordiligi e Dorabella partono.)
(The ladies leave.)

ALFONSO
Non son cattivo comico, va bene: Al concertato loco
I'm not (a) bad actor! Well: At the agreed place

i due campioni di Ciprigna e di Marte
the two champions of Venus and of Mars
(the two champions of love and war)

mi staranno attendendo: or senza indugio
will be for me waiting. Now without delay

raggiungerli conviene. Quante smorfie…quante buffonerie…
to meet them I must go. What grimaces…what playacting…

tanto meglio per me, cadran più facilmente:
so much the better for me, they will fall more easily:

Questa razza di gente è la più presta
This sort of people is the most swift

a cangiarsi d'umore.
to change their mood.

Oh poverini, per femmina giocar cento zecchini?
Oh, poor devils, for (a) woman wager a hundred sequins?

"Nel mare solca, e nell'arena semina,
"In the sea ploughs and in the sand sows,

e il vago vento spera in rete accogliere
and the wild wind hopes in net to catch,

chi fonda sue speranze in cor di femmina."
who bases his hopes on (the) heart of woman."
("Rather plough the sea, sow in sand or try to catch the wild wind
with a net than place your hopes on the heart of a woman.")

*(Camera con tre porte. Despina presenta il cioccolatte sopra una
guantiera.)*
*(In an elegant room in Fiordiligi's and Dorabella's home there are several
chairs and a small table. Despina is preparing some chocolate.)*

DESPINA

Che vita maledetta è il far la cameriera;
What life accursed is it to be the maid;

Dal mattino alla sera si fa, si suda, si lavora,
From morning to evening we do, we sweat, we work,

e poi di tanto che si fa nulla è per noi.
and after so much that we do, nothing is for us.

È mezz'ora che sbatto, il cioccolatte è fatto,
It's half an hour that I'm whipping, the chocolate is done,

ed a me tocca restar ad odorarlo a secca bocca.
and to me is left to smell it with dry mouth.
(and all that's left for me to do is smell it without tasting it.)

Non è forse la mia come la vostra? O garbate Signore,
Isn't maybe mine like yours? Oh, gracious ladies,
(Isn't my mouth the same as yours? Oh gracious ladies,)

chi a voi dessi l'essenza, e a me l'odore?
that to you should be given the flavor and to me the smell?
(why should you get the flavor and I only the smell?)

Per Bacco, vo' assaggiarlo. Com'è buono!
By Bacchus, I'll taste it: how it is good!
(By Jove, let me taste it…how delicious!)

(Si forbe la bocca.)
(She wipes her mouth.)

Vien gente; o ciel, son le padrone!
Come people; oh heaven, it's the mistresses.
(Someone is coming; oh heaven, it's my mistresses!)

(Entrano Fiordiligi e Dorabella.)
(Fiordiligi and Dorabella enter in a state of desperate agitation.)

DESPINA
(presentando il cioccolatte sopra una guantiera)
(placing the chocolate on a tray)
Madame, ecco la vostra colazione. Diamine,[15] cosa fate?
My ladies, here is your breakfast. Good grief! What are you doing?

(Dorabella gitta tutto a terra. Si cavano entrambe tutti gli ornamenti donneschi.)
(Both women divest themselves of their feminine accessories and throw them on the floor.)

DORABELLA
Ah!

FIORDILIGI
Ah!

DESPINA
Che cosa è nato?
What thing is born?[16]
(What happened?)

FIORDILIGI
Ov'è un acciaro, un veleno dov'è?
Where is a sword, a poison where is it?

DESPINA
Padrone, dico…
(My) ladies, I say…

NO. 11 ARIA

DORABELLA
Ah, scostati, paventa il tristo effetto
Ah, get away from me, beware the sad consequence

d'un disperato affetto! Chiudi quelle finestre…
of a desperate love! Shut those windows…

Odio la luce, odio l'aria che spiro, odio me stessa…
I hate the light, I hate the air that I breathe, I hate myself…

Chi schernisce il mio duol, chi mi consola?
Who mocks my grief, who can console me?

Deh fuggi, per pietà, fuggi, lasciami sola.
Please go away for pity's sake, go away, leave me alone.

Smanie implacabili che m'agitate
Torments implacable that agitate me,

dentro quest'anima più non cessate
inside this soul no more cease,

finché l'angoscia mi fa morir.
until my anguish makes me die.
(Implacable torments, don't cease to agitate my soul until this anguish makes me die.)

Esempio misero d'amor funesto
(An) example miserable of a love tragic

darò all'Eumenidi se viva resto,
I shall give the Eumenidies[17] if alive I remain,

col suono orribile de' miei sospir.
with the sound horrible of my sighs.
(If I remain alive I shall give the Eumenidies a miserable example
of a tragic love with the horrible sound of my sighs.)

(Le sorelle cadono sulle sedie.)
(Both women collapse in their chairs in utter despair.)

DESPINA
Signora Dorabella, Signora Fiordiligi, ditemi, che cosa è stato?
Miss Dorabella, Miss Fiordiligi, tell me what has happened?

DORABELLA
Oh, terribil disgrazia!
Oh, (a) terrible disaster!

DESPINA
Sbrigatvi in buon'ora.
Out with it, quickly.
(Tell me then, quickly.)

FIORDILIGI
Da Napoli partiti sono gli amanti nostri.
From Naples gone are the lovers ours.
(Our lovers have left Naples.)

DESPINA
(ridendo)
(laughing)
Non c'è altro? Ritorneran.
Isn't there anything else? They will return.
(Is that all? They will return.)

DORABELLA
Chi sa!
Who knows!

DESPINA
Come, chi sa, dove son iti?
How who knows? Where have they gone?
(What do you mean, who knows? Where have they gone?)

DORABELLA
Al campo di battaglia.
To the field of battle.

DESPINA
Tanto meglio per loro: li vedrete tornar carchi d'alloro.
So much the better for them. You'll see them return laden with
laurels.

FIORDILIGI
Ma ponno[18] anche perir.
But they can also perish.

DESPINA
Allora poi, tanto meglio per voi.
Then afterwards, so much the better for you.
(In that case, so much the better for you.)

FIORDILIGI
(sorge arrabbiata)
(rising angrily)
Sciocca, che dici?
Stupid girl, what are you saying?

DESPINA
La pura verità, due ne perdete, vi restan tutti gli altri.
The pure truth. Two (men) you lose, there are left to you all the others.
(The plain truth: You lose two, you've got all the others left.)

FIORDILIGI
Ah, perduto Guglielmo mi pare ch'io morrei!
Ah, lost Guglielmo I think that I would die!
(Ah, if Guglielmo were lost, I think I would die!)

DORABELLA
Ah, Ferrando perduto, mi par che viva a seppellirmi andrei!
Ah, Ferrando lost, I think that alive to bury myself I'd go!
(Ah, if Ferrando were lost, I think I'd bury myself alive!)

DESPINA
Brave, "vi par," ma non è ver:
Good for you! "You think so," but it isn't true.

Ancora non vi fu donna che d'amor sia morta.
Yet there hasn't been (a) woman who from love has died.
(There hasn't been a woman yet who has died of love.)

Per un uomo morir! Altri ve n'anno che compensano il danno.
For a man to die! Others there are who reward the damage.
(To die for a man! There are plenty others who'll console you for your loss.)

DORABELLA
E credi che potria altr'uomo amar
And do you believe that could another man love

chi s'ebbe per amante un Guglielmo, un Ferrando?
who had for lover a Guglielmo, a Ferrando?
(And do you believe that women who had for lovers a Guglielmo
or a Ferrando could ever love another man?)

DESPINA
Han gli altri ancora tutto quello ch'han essi;
Have the others also everything that have they;
(The other men have everything that your lovers have;)

Un uom adesso amate, un'altro n'amerete:
A man now you love, another you will love.

Uno val l'altro,
One is worth (as much as) the other,

perché nessun val nulla;
because not one is worth anything;

Ma non parliam di ciò, sono ancor vivi e vivi torneran:
But let's not talk of that. They're still alive and alive they'll return;

Ma son lontani, e piuttosto che in vani pianti
But they're far away, and rather than in useless tears

perdere il tempo, pensate a divertirvi.
to waste your time, think of amusing yourselves.

FIORDILIGI
(con rabbia)
(angrily)
Divertirci?
Amuse ourselves?

DESPINA
Sicuro, e quel ch'è meglio, far all'amor come assassine,
Certainly, and what's even better, make love like murderesses,[19]

e come faranno al campo i vostri cari amanti.
as will do in the battlefield your dear lovers.
(just as your dear lovers will on the battlefield.)

DORABELLA
Non offender così quelle alme belle, di fedeltà,
Don't offend thus those souls lovely of faithfulness,

d'intatto amore esempi.
of chaste love examples!
(Don't offend those fair souls like that, for they are examples of
chaste love and faithfulness!)

DESPINA
Via, via! Passaro i tempi
Go on! Have passed the times

da spacciar queste favole ai bambini.
of circulating these fairy tales to children!
(Go on! The days are past when such fairy tales could be told, even
to children!)

NO. 12 ARIA

In uomini, in soldati, sperare fedeltà?
In men, in soldiers, to hope for faithfulness?

Non vi fate sentir, per carità![20]
Don't let yourselves be heard, for charity!
(Don't let anyone hear you, for pity's sake!)

Di pasta simile son tutti quanti,
Of stuff same are all of them,
(They're all made of the same stuff,)

Le fronde mobili, l'aure incostanti
The leaves quivering, the breezes fickle

han più degli uomini stabilità.
have more than men stability.
(The quivering leaves and fickle breezes have more constancy than men.)

Mentite lagrime, fallaci sguardi, voci ingannevoli,
Lying tears, false glances, voices deceitful,

vezzi bugiardi, son le primarie lor qualità.
charms lying, are the primary their qualities.
(Their primary qualities are lying tears, false glances, deceitful voices and lying charms.)

In noi non amano che il lor diletto,
In us they don't love but their pleasure,
(They do not love us except for their own pleasure,)

poi ci dispregiano, neganci affetto,
then they despise us, deny us affection,

né val da' barbari chieder pietà.
nor (is it) worth from barbarians to ask for mercy.
(You might as well ask a barbarian for mercy.)
(It's no use begging a barbarian for pity.)

Paghiam, o femmine, d'ugual moneta
Let us pay, oh women, with the same coin

questa malefica razza indiscreta
this evil breed indiscreet;
(Oh women, let us repay this evil breed of indiscreet men with the
same coin;)

Amiam per comodo, per vanità, la ra la la.
Let us love for convenience, for vanity, la ra la la.
(Let us love at our convenience, for our vanity! La ra la la!)

(Tutte partono. Entra Don Alfonso.)
(The ladies leave. Immediately after, Don Alfonso enters.)

ALFONSO
Che silenzio, che aspetto di tristezza spirano queste stanze!
What silence, what look of sadness breathe these rooms!

Poverette, non han già tutto il torto:
Poor girls! They don't have now entirely the blame:
(Poor girls! They are not entirely to blame:)

Bisogna consolarle. Infin che vanno i due creduli sposi,
I must console them. While go the two credulous fiancés

com'io loro commisi, a mascherarsi,
as I them ordered, to disguise themselves
(I must console them. While the two credulous fiancés go to disguise
themselves as I ordered them)

pensiam cosa può farsi.
let me think what can be done.

Temo un po' per Despina: quella furba potrebbe riconoscerli,
I fear a bit for Despina: That sly one could recognize them,

potrebbe rovesciarmi le macchine.[21] Vedremo…
she could upset me the machinery. Let's see…
(she could upset my well-laid plans. Let's see…)

Se mai farà bisogno un regaletto a tempo:
If ever it was needed, a little gift in (good) time:

Un zecchinetto per una cameriera è un gran scongiuro.
A little sequin for a chambermaid is a big charm.
(A little gold piece for a chambermaid would work like a charm.)

Ma per esser sicuro, si potria metterla in parte
But to be sure I could let her in on, little by little

a parte del secreto. Eccellente è il progetto…
as part of the secret…Excellent is the idea…

La sua camera è questa:
Her room is this one:

(Egli bussa.)
(He knocks.)

Despinetta![22]

DESPINA
Chi batte?
Who is knocking?

ALFONSO
Oh!

DESPINA
(entrando)
(entering)
Ih!

ALFONSO
Despina mia, di te bisogno avrei.
Despina mine, of you need I would have.
(My Despina, I need you.)

DESPINA
Ed io niente di voi.
And I nothing from you.
(And I need nothing from you.)

ALFONSO
Ti vo' fare del ben.
I want to do you some good.
(I want to do something good for you.)
(I want to do you a favor.)

DESPINA
A una fanciulla un vechio come lei
For a young girl an old man like you

non può far nulla.
cannot do anything.

ALFONSO
(mostrandole una moneta d'oro)
(showing her a gold coin)
Parla piano ed osserva.
Speak softly and observe.

DESPINA
Me la dona?
Are you giving it to me?

ALFONSO
Sì, se meco[23] sei buona.
Yes, if with me you're good.

DESPINA
E che vorrebbe? È l'oro il mio giulebbe.
And what would you want? Is gold my weakness.[24]
(And what is it that you want? Gold is my weakness.)

ALFONSO
Ed oro avrai; ma ci vuol fedeltà.
And gold you shall have; but I need (your) loyalty.

DESPINA
Non c'è altro? Son qua.
Is there nothing else? I'm here.
(Is that all? I'm here at your service.)

ALFONSO
(dandole una moneta)
(giving her a coin)

Prendi ed ascota: Sai che le tue padrone
Take it and listen: You know that your mistresses

han perduti gli amanti.
have lost their lovers.

DESPINA
Lo so.
I know it.

ALFONSO
Tutti i lor pianti, tutti i deliri loro ancor tu sai.
All their tears, all the ravings theirs also you know.
(And you've heard all their weeping and raving.)

DESPINA
So tutto.
I know everything.

ALFONSO
Orben; se mai per consolarle un poco,
Well now, if perhaps, to console them a little

e trar come diciam, chiodo per chiodo,[25]
and drive out, as we say, a nail with (another) nail,

tu ritrovassi il modo da metter in lor grazia
you could find the way to introduce to their (good) graces,

due soggetti di garbo, che vorrieno provar...
two gentlemen of elegance who would want to try...

già mi capisci...C'è una mancia per te di venti scudi,
already you understand me...There's a tip of twenty crowns

se li fai riuscir.
if you make them succeed.

DESPINA
Non mi dispiace questa proposizione.
It doesn't displease me, this proposition.

Ma con quelle buffone...Basta, udite:
But with those silly girls...Enough, listen:

Son giovani? Son belli? E sopra tutto
Are they young? Are they handsome? And above all

hanno una buona borsa i vostri concorrenti?
have they a good purse your candidates?
(are your candidates rich?)

ALFONSO
Han tutto quello che piacer può a due donne di giudizio.
They have everything that please can two women of discernment.
(They have everything that can please two discerning women.)

DESPINA
E dove son?
And where are they?

ALFONSO
Son lì. Li posso far entrar?
They're there. May I let them enter?
(They're outside. May I let them in?)

DESPINA
Direi di sì.
I should say so.

(Entrano Ferrando e Guglielmo, che son travestiti.)
(Don Alfonso brings in the two disguised young men.)

NO. 13 SESTETTO
NO. 13 SEXTET

ALFONSO
Alla bella Despinetta vi presento, amici miei:
To the lovely Despinetta I introduce you, friends mine:

non dipende che da lei consolar il vostro cor.
It doesn't depend but from her to console your heart.
(The consolation of your hearts depends solely on her.)

FERRANDO, GUGLIELMO
Per la man, che lieto io bacio,
By this hand that happily I kiss,

per quei rai di grazia pieni,
by those eyes with grace filled,

fa' che volga a me sereni
make that she turn to me serene

i begli occhi il mio tesor.
her lovely eyes my treasure.
(By this hand that I kiss with joy, by those eyes full of charm, may
my treasure turn her serene gaze upon me.)

DESPINA
(a parte)
(to herself, laughing)
Che sembianze! Che vestiti! Che figure!
What faces! What clothes! What appearance!

Che mustacchi! Io non so se son Vallacchi,
What mustachios! I don't know if they're Walachians[26]

o se turchi son costor.
or if Turks are they.
(I can't tell if they're Walachians or Turks.)

ALFONSO
Che ti par di quell'aspetto?
What do you think of their looks?

DESPINA
(piano a Alfonso)
(softly, to Alfonso)
Per parlarvi schietto, schietto, hanno un muso fuor dell'uso,
To speak to you frankly, they have a mug out of the ordinary,[27]
(To be frank, they've got peculiar faces,)

vero antidoto d'amor.
(a) true antidote to love.

FERRANDO, GUGLIELMO
(Or la cosa è appien decisa:
(Now the matter is fully settled:

se costei non ci ravvisa
if she doesn't recognize us

ALFONSO
Se constei non *li* ravvisa
If she doesn't recognize *them*

FERRANDO, GUGLIELMO, ALFONSO
Non c'è più nessun timor.)
There's no more any fear.)
(There's no need to worry.)

FIORDILIGI, DORABELLA
(dietro le quinte)
(from inside)
Ehi, Despina! Olà, Despina!
Hey, Despina! Ho there, Despina!

DESPINA
Le padrone!
My mistresses!

ALFONSO
(a Despina)
(to Despina)
Ecco l'istante! Fa con arte: io qui m'ascondo.
Here's the moment! Act with art: I here will hide.
(Here's the moment! Use your wits. I'll hide here.)

FIORDILIGI, DORABELLA
(entrando)
(entering)
Ragazzaccia[28] tracotante, che fai lì con simil gente?
Gutter-snipe arrogant, what are you doing there with such people?
(You arrogant little gutter-snipe, what are you doing there with such people!)

Falli uscire immantinente, o ti fo pentir con lor.
Make them leave immediately, or I'll make you regret with them.
(Make them leave immediately or all of you will regret it.)

DESPINA, FERRANDO, GUGLIELMO
(tutti e tre s'inginocchiano)
(kneeling)
Ah, madame, perdonate! Al bel piè languir mirate
Ah, ladies, forgive us! At your lovely feet languishing see

due meschin di vostro metro spasimanti adorator.
two wretches, of your charms ardent adorers.
(two wretches who ardently adore your charms.)

FIORDILIGI, DORABELLA
Giusti Numi! Cosa sento?
Merciful gods! What do I hear?

Dell'enorme tradimento chi fu mai l'indegno autor?
Of this enormous betrayal who was the worthless author?
(Who was the worthless perpetrator of this enormous betrayal?)

DESPINA, FERRANDO. GUGLIELMO
Deh, calmate quello sdegno...
Please, calm your indignation...

FIORDILIGI, DORABELLA
Ah, che più non ho ritegno!
Ah, that no longer I have control!
(Ah, I am losing my control!)

Tutta piena ho l'alma in petto di dispetto e di furor!
All full I have my soul in my breast of disgust and with fury!
(My soul is filled with annoyance and fury!)

FERRANDO, GUGLIELMO
Qual diletto è a questo petto quella rabbia e quel furor!
What delight is to my heart that rage and that fury!

DESPINA, ALFONSO
(una questi ultimi dallo sportello)
(the latter from the door)
Mi dà un poco di sospetto quella rabbia e quel furor!
It gives me a bit of suspicion that rage and that fury!
(Their fury and rage make me somewhat suspicious!)

(Don Alfonso entrando.)
(Don Alfonso pretends as if he is entering.)

ALFONSO
Che sussurro! Che strepito! Che scompiglio è mai questo?
What a noise! What uproar! What disturbance is this?

Siete pazze, care le mie ragazze?
Are you crazy, dear (my) young girls?

Volete sollevar il vicinato? Cosa avete? Ch'è nato?
Do you wish to rouse the neighbors? What's wrong? What happened?

DORABELLA
(con rabbia)
(angrily)
Oh ciel! Mirate! Uomini in casa nostra!
Oh heaven! Look! Men in house ours!
(Oh heaven! Look! Men in our house!)

ALFONSO
(senza guardarli)
(without looking at them)
Che male c'è?
What is wrong with that?

FIORDILIGI
(eccitato)
(excitedly)
Che male? In questo giorno? Dopo il caso funesto?
What is wrong? On this day? After the event tragic?

ALFONSO
(fingendo di riconoscere due amici a lungo perduto)
(pretending to recognize two long-lost friends)
Stelle! Sogno, o son desto? Amici miei, miei dolcissimi amici!
Stars! Am I dreaming or am I awake? My friends, my sweetest
friends!

Voi qui? Come? In qual modo? Numi! Quanto ne godo!
You here? How? In what way? Gods! How delighted I am!

(a parte a Ferrando e Guglielmo)
(softly to the two men)

Secondatemi.
Back me up.

FERRANDO
Amico Don Alfonso!
Friend Don Alfonso!

GUGLIELMO
Amico caro!
Friend dear!
(My dear friend!)

(Si abbracciano con trasporto.)
(They embrace each other eagerly.)

ALFONSO
Oh bella improvvisata!
What (a) lovely surprise!

DESPINA
(a Don Alfonso)
(to Don Alfsonso)
Li conoscete voi?
Them know you?
(Do you know them?)

ALFONSO
Se li conosco! Questi sono i più dolci amici
If I know them! These are the most sweet friends

ch'io m'abbia in questo mondo, e vostri ancor saranno.
that I could have in this world, and yours also they will be.

FIORDILIGI
E in casa mia che fanno?
And in (the) house mine what are they doing?

GUGLIELMO
Ai vostri piedi due rei, due delinquenti,
At your feet two culprits, two delinquents,

ecco, madame! Amor…
behold, my ladies! Love…

FIORDILIGI
Numi! Che sento!
Gods! What do I hear!

Leontyne Price as Fiordiligi, 1965
Louis Mélançon/Metropolitan Opera Archives

Teresa Stratas as Despina and Rosalind Elias as Dorabella, 1971

David Rendall as Ferrando and James Morris as Guglielmo, 1982
METROPOLITAN OPERA ARCHIVE

Kiri Te Kanawa as Fiordiligi and Maria Ewing as Dorabella, 1982
METROPOLITAN OPERA ARCHIVES

Kiri Te Kanawa as Fiordiligi, 1988

Håkan Hagegård as Guglielmo, 1988

Dawn Upshaw as Despina, 1988

Jerry Hadley as Ferrando and Thomas Hampson as
Guglielmo, 1990

Tatiana Troyanos as Dorabella, 1990

Carol Vaness as Fiordiligi, 1991
METROPOLITAN OPERA ARCHIVES

FERRANDO
Amor, il Nume sì possente, per voi qui ci conduce.
Love, the god so powerful, for you here us leads.
(The all-powerful god of love brings us here for you.)

(Le donne si ritirano, essi le inseguono.)
(The girls retreat, pursued avidly by the two swains.)

GUGLIELMO
Vista appena la luce di vostre fulgidissime pupille…
Seen barely the light from your gleaming pupils…
(No sooner did we see the light from your gleaming eyes…)

FERRANDO
Che alle vive faville…
Than at the lively sparks…

GUGLIELMO
Farfallette amorose, e agonizzanti…
Little moths loving dying…
(Like two lovesick, agonizing moths…)

FERRANDO
Vi voliamo davanti…
To you we flutter in front…
(We come fluttering before you…)

GUGLIELMO
Ed ai lati, ed a retro…
And at your sides, and at (your) back…

FERRANDO, GUGLIELMO
Per implorar pietade in flebil metro!
To implore (for) pity in plaintive meter![29]

FIORDILIGI
Stelle! Che ardir!
Stars! What daring!

DORABELLA
Sorella, che facciamo?
Sister, what shall we do?

*(**Despina sorte impaurita.**)*
(Despina leaves in a fright.)

FIORDILIGI
Temerari! Sortite fuori di questo loco!
Rash ones! Get out of this place!

E non profani l'alito infausto degl'infami detti
And let it not profane the breath noxious of your evil words

nostro cor, nostro orecchio, e nostri affetti!
our heart, our ear, and our affections!
(And may the noxious breath of your evil words not profane our
hearts, our ears and our affections!)

Invan per voi, per gli altri invan
In vain for you, for others (also) in vain

si cerca le nostre alme sedur:
you may seek our souls to seduce:
(In vain may you, or any other men, seek to seduce our souls.)

L'intatta fede che per noi già si diede ai cari amanti,
The intact fidelity which by us already has been given to our dear
lovers

saprem loro serbar infino a morte,
we'll know how to for them keep unto death,

a dispetto del mondo e della sorte.
defying the world and fate.
(Our unsullied fidelity which we have already given to our lovers will be kept for them even unto death, in spite of the world and fate itself.)

NO. 14 ARIA

FIORDILIGI
Come scoglio immoto resta contro i venti e la tempesta,
As a reef immovable stays against the winds and the tempest,

così ognor quest'alma è forte nella fede e nell'amor.
so always my soul is strong in loyalty and in love.

Con noi nacque quella face che ci piace e ci consola;
With us began that torch that pleases us and consoles us;
(A fire was kindled in us that brings us pleasure and comfort;)

e potrà la morte sola far che cangi affetto il cor.
and can death only cause that change affection the heart.
(and only death can make us change the affections of our hearts.)

Rispettate, anime[30] ingrate, questo esempio di costanza,
Respect, souls ungrateful, this example of constancy
(You miserable souls, respect our example of constancy)

e una barbara speranza non vi renda audaci ancor.
and a barbarous hope not make you bold again.
(and may you not be emboldened again by outrageous hope.)

(Le donne vanno per partire.)
(The girls start to leave, but Ferrando and Guglielmo stop them.)

FERRANDO
(a Fiordiligi)
(to Fiordiligi)
Ah, non partite!
Ah, don't leave!

GUGLIELMO
(a Dorabella)
(to Dorabella)
Ah, barbara, restate!
Ah, cruel one, stay!

(a parte a Don Alfonso)
(to Alfonso)

Che vi pare?
What do you think?

ALFONSO
(a parte a Guglielmo)
(softly, to Guglielmo)
(Aspettate.)
(Wait.)

(alle donne)
(aloud to the girls)

Per carità, ragazze, non mi fate più far trista figura.
For pity's sake, girls, don't make me any more make bad figure.[31]
(Please, girls, don't make me look bad any more!)

DORABELLA
(con fuoco)
(with pique)
E che pretendereste?
And what do you expect?

ALFONSO
Eh, nulla…ma mi pare che un pochin di dolcezza…
Oh! nothing…but it seems to me that a little kindness…

Alfin, son galantuomini e sono amici miei.
After all, they're gentlemen and they're friends of mine.

FIORDILIGI
Come! E udire dovrei…
What! And listen I must…

GUGLIELMO
Le nostre pene e sentirne pieta!
Our sufferings and feel for them pity!
(You must listen to our sufferings and feel pity for them!)

La celeste beltà degli occhi vostri
The celestial beauty of the eyes yours

la piaga apriì nei nostri
the wound opened in us
(The celestial beauty of your eyes opened up a wound in us)

cui rimediar può solo il balsamo d'amore:
which heal can only the balm of love.
(which only the balm of love can heal.)

Un solo istante il core aprite, o belle,
One just moment the heart open, oh fair ones,

a sue dolci facelle, o a voi davanti
to its bright lights, or to you before
(Just open your hearts to its bright light for one moment, oh fair
ones, or before you)

spirar vedrete i più fedeli amanti.
expire you will see the most faithful lovers.
(you will see these most faithful lovers die.)

NO. 15 ARIA

GUGLIELMO
Non siate ritrosi, occhietti vezzosi,
Don't be shy, little eyes pretty,

due lampi amorosi vibrate un po' qua.
two flashing glances loving send a bit here.
(Don't be shy, pretty eyes. Send two loving, flashing glances in our
direction.)

Felici rendeteci, amate con noi,
Happy make us, love with us,

e noi felicissime faremo anche voi.
and we most happy will make also you.
(Love us, make us happy and we in turn will make you very happy.)

Guardate, toccate, il tutto osservate;
Look, touch, everything observe;

Siam due cari matti, siam forti e ben fatti,
We're two dear madmen, we're strong and well built,

e come ognun vede, sia merto, sia caso,
and as everyone can see, be it merit, be it chance,

abbiamo bel piede, bell'occhio, bel naso,
we have lovely feet, lovely eyes, (a) fine nose,

Toaccate, il tutto osservate.

E questi mustacchi chiamare si possono
And these mustaches call themselves can
(And these mustaches can be called)

trionfi degli uomini, pennacchi d'amor.
triumphs of manhood, fancy feathers of love.

Trionfi, pennacchi, mustacchi! [32]

NOTE: For the first performance of the opera, Mozart had written another bigger and longer aria for Guglielmo at this point, which is included below. It has been performed, on occasion, in place of No. 15 above ("Non siate ritrosi"), which is a shorter aria Mozart felt "would not disturb the flow of the action towards its conclusion with the finale of Act I." This aria, "Rivolgete a lui lo sguardo," is now given Köchel listing K. 584 as a "concert aria."

NO. 15 ARIA

GUGLIELMO
(a Fiordiligi)
(to Fiordiligi)

Rivolgete a lui lo sguardo, e vedrete come sta;

Turn to him your gaze, and you will see what he looks like;

Tutto dice "Io gelo…io ardo, idol mio, pieta."

Everything (in him) speaks "I am freezing…I am burning, idol mine, pity."

(Look at Ferrando, everything in him speaks "I'm burning, I'm freezing, my beloved have pity on me.")

(a Dorabella)

(to Dorabella)

E voi cara un sol momento

And you, dearest, one sole moment

il bel diglio a me volgete,

your lovely eyes to me turn,

(and you, dearest one, turn your eyes to me for one sole moment,)

e nel mio ritroverete quell che il labbro dir non sa.

and in mine you'll find that which the lip say cannot.

(and in my eyes you will see what my lips can't say.)

Un Orlando[33] innamorato non è niente in mio confronto;

An Orlando in love isn't anything compared to me;

(An Orlando in love is nothing compared to me;)

D'un Medoro il sen piagato

Of a Medoro the breast wounded

verso lui per mulla io conto.

against him for nothing I count.

(I count my suffering as nothing compared to Medoro's.)

Son di fuoco I miei sospiri,
Are of fire my sighs,

son di bronzo I miei[34] desiri.
are of bronze my desires.
(My sighs are fiery and my desires are hard as bronze.)[35]

Se si parla poi di metro,
If one talks then of merit,

certo io sono, ed egli è certo,
certain I am and it is true,

che gli uguali non si trovano da Vienna al Canadà:
that the equals can't be found from Vienna to Canada.
(If one talks of merit, I am sure that an equal to myself cannot be
found from Vienna to Canada.)

Siam due cresi per ricchezza,
We're two Croesus by (our) riches,
(We're rich like two Croesus[36])

due Narcisi per ballezza.
two Narcissus by (our) beauty.
(and beautiful like Narcissus.[37])

In amor i Marcantoni verso noi sarian buffoni.
In love the Marc Anthonys compared to us would be buffoons.
(In love, all the Marc Anthonys of the world would be mere
buffoons.)

Siam più forti d'un Ciclopo
We're stronger than Cyclops[38]

letterati al par d'Esopo:
literate on a par with Aesop;

Se balliamo, un Pich ne cede,
When we dance, a Pich[39] yields to us,

sì gentil e snello è il piede.
so graceful and slim is our foot.

So cantiam, col trillo solo
When we sing, with the trill alone

facciam torto al'usignolo;
we do wrong to the nightingale.
(we outsing the nightingale.)

E qualch'altro capitale abbiam noi che alcun non sa.
And some other assets have we that no one knows.
(And we have some other assets that no one knows about.)[40]

(Fiordiligi e Dorabella partono.)
(The two sisters leave in a huff.)

Bella, bella! Tengon sodo; se ne vanno ed io ne godo!
Lovely! Lovely! They're holding firm; they're leaving and I love it!

Eroine di costanza, specchi son di fedeltà.
Heroines of constancy, mirrors they are of faithfulness.
(Those women are heroines of constancy, true mirrors of fidelity!)

(Ferrando e Guglielmo, appena soli con Don Alfonso, ridono.)
(Ferrando and Guglielmo start to laugh.)

NO. 16 TERZETTO
NO. 16 TRIO

ALFONSO
E voi ridete?
And you are laughing?

FERRANDO, GUGLIELMO
(ride fragorosamente)
(laughing uproariously)
Certo, ridiamo.
Certainly, we're laughing!

ALFONSO
Ma cosa avete?
But what's the matter?

FERRANDO, GUGLIELMO
Già lo sappiamo.
Already we know.
(We know already.)

ALFONSO
Ridete piano!
Laugh quietly!

FERRANDO, GUGLIELMO
Parlate in vano!
You're talking in vain!

ALFONSO
Se vi sentissero, se vi scoprissero,
If they heard you, if they found you out,

si guasterebbe tutto l'affar. Mi fa da ridere
it would spoil the whole business. It makes me laugh

questo lor ridere, ma so che in piangere dee terminar.
this their laughing, but I know that in weeping it must end.

FERRANDO, GUGLIELMO
Ah, che dal ridere l'alma dividere,
Ah, but from laughing my soul divides,
(My sides are splitting from laughter,)

ah, che le viscere sento scoppiar!
ah, but my insides I feel bursting!

ALFONSO
Si può sapere un poco la cagion di quel riso?
Can I know a little the reason for that laughter?
(May I inquire the reason for this laughter?)

GUGLIELMO
Oh, cospettaccio! Non vi pare che abbiam giusta ragione,
Oh, darn it all! Don't you think that we have just reasons,

il mio caro padrone?
my dear master?

FERRANDO
(scherzosamente)
(jokingly)
Quanto pagar volete, e a monte è la scommessa?
How much pay do you wish, and forfeited is the bet?
(How much do you want to pay us, now that the bet is forfeited?)

GUGLIELMO
(scherzosamente)
(jokingly)
Pagate la metà!
Pay us half!

FERRANDO
Pagate solo ventiquattro zecchini.
Pay us only twenty-four sequins!

ALFONSO
Poveri innocentini, venite qua:
Poor innocent little boys, come here:

Vi voglio porre il ditino in bocca.
You I want to put the little finger in mouth.
(Let me stick your little finger in your mouth.)[41]

GUGLIELMO
E avete ancora coraggio di fiatar?
And you have still (the) courage to breathe?

ALFONSO
Avanti sera ci parlerem.
Before evening we will talk.

FERRANDO
Quando volete!
Whatever you wish!

ALFONSO
Intanto, silenzio e ubbidienza fino a doman mattina.
In the meanwhile, silence and obedience until tomorrow morning.

GUGLIELMO
Siamo soldati e amiam la disciplina.
We're soldiers and we love discipline.

ALFONSO
Orbene: andate un poco ad attendermi entrambi
Now then, go for a while to wait for me both of you

in giardinetto. Colà vi manderò gli ordini miei.
in the little garden. There I will send you the orders mine.

GUGLIELMO
Ed oggi non si mangia?
And today aren't we eating?

FERRANDO
Cosa serve? A battaglia finita
What for? Once (the) battle (is) ended

fia la cena per noi più saporita.
be the supper for us tastier.
(What for? Once this battle is over, we can truly relish our supper…)

NO. 17 ARIA

FERRANDO
Un'aura amorosa del nostro tesoro
A breath of love from our treasure
(A loving breath from our sweethearts)

un dolce ristoro al cor porgerà.
a sweet refreshment to our heart will bring.

Al cor che nudrito da speme d'amore
The heart that (is) nourished by hope, by love,

di un'esca migliore bisogno non ha.
of a nourishment better need has not.
(has no need of better food.)

ALFONSO
Oh, la saria da ridere: sì poche sono le donne costanti
Oh, it makes me laugh, so few are the women constant

in questo mondo e qui ve ne son due!
in this world and here there are two of them!
(This is laughable! There are so few faithful women in this world
and here we have two of them!)

Non sarà nulla...
That cannot be...

(Despina entra.)
(Despina enters.)

Vieni, fanciulla, e dimmi un poco
Come, girl, and tell me (a bit)

dove son e che fan le tue padrone.
where they are and what they're doing, your mistresses.

DESPINA
Le povere buffone stanno nel giardinetto
The poor silly girls are in the small garden

a lagnarsi coll'aria e colle mosche
bemoaning with the air and with the flies

d'aver perso gli amanti.
of having lost their lovers.

ALFONSO
E come credi che l'affar finirà?
And how do you think that things will end?
(And how do you think it will turn out?)

Possiam sperare che faranno giudizio?
Do we want to hope that they will come to their senses?

DESPINA
Io lo farei; e dove piangon esse io riderei.
I would do it; and where weep they, I would laugh.
(I would wait and instead of weeping like they do, I'd be laughing.)

Disperarsi, strozzarsi, perché parte un amante?
To despair, to choke oneself because leaves a lover?
(To despair, to choke to death because a lover leaves?)

Guardate che pazzia!
Behold, what madness!

Se ne pigliano due, s'uno va via.
They should take two, if one goes off.
(If one lover goes off, they should take on two others!)

ALFONSO
Brava, questa e purdenza!
Bravo, that is sensible!

(fra sé)
(aside)

(Bisogna impuntigliarla.)
(I must insist with her.)

DESPINA
E leggo di natura e non prudenza sola.
It's (the) law of nature and not prudence alone.
(It's the law of nature, not just being sensible.)

Amor cos'è? Diletto, comodo, gusto, gioia, divertimento, passatempo,
Love, what is it? Pleasure, convenience, taste, joy, diversion, pastime,

allegria: Non è più amore se incomodo diventa,
happiness. It's no longer love if a nuisance it becomes,

se invece di allettar nuoce e tormenta.
if instead of pleasing, annoys and torments.
(Love is no longer love if it becomes a nuisance, if instead of giving
pleasure it gives only annoyance and torment.)

ALFONSO
Ma intanto queste pazze…
But meanwhile these madwomen…

DESPINA
Faranno a modo nostro. È buon che sappiano
They will do as we tell them to. It's good that they should know

d'esser amate da color.[42]
that they're loved by them.

ALFONSO
Lo sanno.
They know it.

DESPINA
Dunque, riameranno.
Then they will love again.

"Diglielo," si suol dire, "e lascia fare il diavolo."
"Tell them," they say, "and let take care the devil."
(There's a saying, "Just say the word and let the devil take care of
it.")

ALFONSO
Ma come far vuoi perchè ritornino,
But how make you want so that they should return,

or che partit sono, e che li sentano
now that gone they are, and that they should listen to them

e tentare si lascino, queste tue bestioline?
and to be tempted they let themselves these your stupid little girls?
(But how will you arrange for them to return, now that they are
gone, and make your stupid little girls listen to them and allow
themselves to be tempted?)

DESPINA
A me lasciate la briga di condur tutta la macchina.
To me leave the trouble of carrying the whole machinery.
(Let me take care of making all the preparations.)

Quando Despina macchina[43] **una cosa**
When Despina machinates something

non può mancar d'effetto.
it cannot lack effect.
(it cannot fail to work.)

Ho già menati mill'uomini pel naso,[44]
I've already led a thousand men by the nose,

Saprò menare due femmine.
I will know (how to) lead two women.

Son ricchi, i due monsù⁴⁵ mustacchi?
Are they rich, the two *messieurs* mustachios?

ALFONSO
Son ricchissimi.
They are very rich.

DESPINA
Dove son?
Where are they?

ALFONSO
Sulla strada attendendo mi stanno.
In the street waiting for me they are.

DESPINA
Ite, e sul fatto per la piccola porta a me riconduceteli.
Go, and at once by the small door to me bring them.

V'aspetto nella camera mia. Purché tutto facciate
I wait for you in the room mine. As long as everything you do

com'io v'ordinerò, pria di domani
as I order you, before morning

i vostri amici canteran vittoria;
your friends will celebrate victory;

ed essi avran il gusto, ed io la gloria.
and they will have the pleasure and I, the glory.

(Partono.)

(They exit and we next find ourselves in a pleasant garden with two grassy banks at the sides. Fiordiligi and Dorabella are sadly bemoaning their fate.)

NO. 18 FINALE

FIORDILIGI, DORABELLA
Ah, che tutto in un momento, si cangiò la sorte mia…
Ah, how all in one moment changed the fate mine…

Ah, che un mar pien di tormento è la vita omai per me.
Ah, what a sea full of torment is life now for me.

Finché meco il caro bene
While with me the dear beloved

mi lasciar le ingrate stelle,
allowed to be with me the cruel stars,
(While the cruel stars permitted me to be with my beloved,)

non sapea cos'eran pene, non sapea languir cos'è.
I didn't know what was grief, I did not know languishing what it is.
(I didn't know the meaning of grief or languishing.)

(Ferrando e Guglielmo si sentono dal di dentro, con Alfonso cercando di refraint orlo di fare qualcosa di disperato.)
(Ferrando and Guglielmo are heard from within, with Alfonso trying to restrain them from doing something desperate.)

FERRANDO, GUGLIELMO
Si mora, sì, si mora, onde appagar le ingrate!
Let me die, yes, let me die, so as to satisfy the cruel ones!

ALFONSO
C'è una speranza ancora, non fate, o Dei, non fate!
There's a hope still, don't do it, oh gods, don't do it!

FIORDILIGI, DORABELLA
Stelle, che grida orribili!
Stars, what cries horrible!

FERRANDO, GUGLIELMO
Lasciatemi!
Let go of me!

ALFONSO
Aspettate!
Wait!

(Ferrando e Guglielmo, portando ciascuno una boccetta, entrano seguiti da Don Alfonso.)
(The two men, followed by Alfonso, now enter upon the scene from outside.)

FERRANDO, GUGLIELMO
L'arsenico mi liberi di tanta crudeltà.
(Let) arsenic deliver us from so much cruelty!

(Bevono e gittan via le boccette; nel voltarsi, vedono le due donne.)
(They gulp down the contents of their vials.)

FIORDILIGI, DORABELLA
Stelle! un velen fu quello?
Stars! A poison was that?
(Heaven! Was that a poison?)

ALFONSO
Veleno buono e bello
A poison good and proper

che ad essi in pochi istanti la vita toglierà.
that to them in a few instants their lives will take away.

FIORDILIGI, DORABELLA
Il tragico spettacolo gelare il cor mi fa.
The tragic spectacle freeze my heart makes.
(This tragic spectacle makes my heart freeze.)

FIORDILIGI, DORABELLA, FERRANDO, GUGLIELMO,
ALFONSO
Ah, che del sole il raggio fosco per me diventa.
Ah, that of the sun the ray dark for me becomes.
(It seems to me the light of the sun has dimmed.)

Tremo, le fibre e l'anima
I tremble, my strength and my soul

par che mancar mi senta,
it seems that failing I feel,
(I tremble and it seems that my strength and spirit are failing me,)

né può la lingua o il labbro accenti articolar.
nor can my tongue or my lip words articlate.
(nor can my tongue and lips articulate any words.)

(Ferrando e Guglielmo cadono sopra i banchi d'erba.)
(Ferrando and Guglielmo fall onto two benches.)

ALFONSO
Giacché a morir vicini sono quei meschinelli,
Since to dying close are those poor wretches,
(Since those poor wretches are so close to death,)

pietade almeno a quelli cercate di mostrar.
pity at least for them try to show.

FIORDILIGI, DORABELLA
Gente, accorrete, gente!
People, come help, people!

Nessuno, o Dio, ci sente! Despina!
No one, oh God, hears us! Despina!

DESPINA
(entra)
(coming in)
Chi mi chiama?
Who calls me?

FIORDILIGI, DORABELLA
Despina!

DESPINA
Cosa vedo! Morti i meschini io credo,
What do I see! Dead the wretches I think,

o prossimi a spirar.
or close to expiring.
(What do I see! I think the wretches are dead or close to it.)

ALFONSO
Ah, che purtroppo è vero! Furenti, disperati,
Ah, for indeed it's true! Raging, despairing,

si sono avvelenati, oh, amore singolar!
they themselves poisoned, oh, love singular!
(they poisoned themselves. Oh, what singular love!)

DESPINA
Abbandonar i miseri saria per voi vergogna:
To abandon the poor creatures would be for you shameful:

soccorrerli bisogna.
to succor them is necessary.
(You must help them.)

FIORDILIGI, DORABELLA, ALFONSO
Cosa possiam mai far?
What can we ever do?
(Whatever can we do?)

DESPINA
Di vita ancor dan segno:
Of life still they give sign:
(They still show signs of life:)

Colle pietose mani fate un po' lor sostegno.
With your merciful hands make a bit them support.
(Give them some support with your merciful hands.)

(a Don Alfonso)
(to Don Alfonso)

E voi con me correte:
And you with me run:

un medico, un antidoto voliamo a ricercar.
a doctor, an antidote let us fly to find.
(We two must hasten to find a doctor or an antidote.)

(Despina e Don Alfonso partono.)
(Despina and Don Alfonso leave.)

FIORDILIGI, DORABELLA
Dei, che cimento è questo!
Gods, what experience is this!

Evento più funesto non si potea trovar!
A situation more tragic would be impossible to find!

FERRANDO, GUGLIELMO
(a parte)
(to themselves)
Più bella commediola non si potea trovar.
A more lovely little comedy would be impossible to find!

(forte)
(The two men heave an exaggerated and dramatic sigh.)

Ah!

FIORDILIGI, DORABELLA
Sospiran gli infelici!
They're sighing, the unhappy creatures!

FIORDILIGI
Che facciamo?
What shall we do?

DORABELLA
Tu che dici?
You, what do you say?

FIORDILIGI
In momenti sì dolente chi potriali abbandonar?
In moments so painful who could them abandon?

DORABELLA
(li avvicina)
(approaching them)
Che figure interessanti!
What faces interesting!

FIORDILIGI
(anche sempre più vicino)
(also getting closer)
Possiam farci un poco avanti.
We can bring ourselves a bit forward.
(We could move a little closer to them.)

DORABELLA
Ha freddissima la testa.
He has very cold the head.
(His head is very cold.)

FIORDILIGI
Fredda, fredda è ancora questa.
Cold, cold is also this one.

DORABELLA
Ed il polso?
And his pulse?

FIORDILIGI
Io non gliel' sento.
I not his it feel.
(I can't feel it.)

DORABELLA
Questo batte lento.
This one beats slowly.

FIORDILIGI, DORABELLA
Ah, se tarda ancor l'aita, speme più non v'è di vita.
Ah, if delays more the help hope more there isn't of life.
(If help is delayed much longer all hope of life will be gone.)

FERRANDO, GUGLIELMO
(a parte)
(to themselves)
(Più domestiche e trattabili sono entrambe diventate.)
(More subdued and amenable have both become.)
(Both have become more subdued and amenable.)

Sta a veder che lor pietade va in amore a terminar.
One can see that their pity goes in love to end.
(You'll see how their pity turns to love.)

FIORDILIGI, DORABELLA
Poverini! La lor morte mi farebbe lagrimar,
Poor things! Their death would make me weep.

(Entra Despina travestita da medico, con Don Alfonso.)
(Alfonso brings in Despina, disguised as a doctor.)

ALFONSO
Eccovi il medico, signore belle.
Here's the doctor, ladies fair.

FERRANDO, GUGLIELMO
(Despina in maschera, che trista pelle!)
(Despina in disguise, what ugly skin!)
(Despina in disguise, what a sorry sight!)

DESPINA
Salvete amabiles bonae puellae.[46]
LATIN: Greetings, pleasant good girls!

FIORDILIGI, DORABELLA
Parla un linguaggio che non sappiamo.
He speaks a language that we don't know.

DESPINA
Come comandano dunque parliamo:
As you command then we will speak:

So il greco e l'arabo
I know Greek and Arabic,

so il turco e il vandalo,
I know Turkish and Vandal,

lo svevo e il tartaro so ancor parlar.
Swabian and Tartar I know also to speak.

ALFONSO
Tanti linguaggi per sé conservi.
All those languages to yourself keep.

Quei miserabili per ora osservi:
Those miserable ones for now observe:
(Keep all those languages to yourself; look at those miserable wretches:)

FIORDILIGI, DORABELLA, ALFONSO
Preso hanno il tossico,[47] che si può far?
Taken they have some poison, what can we do?

DESPINA
(toccando il polso e la fronte all'uno ed all'altro)
(taking their pulse and touching their foreheads)
Saper bisognami pria la cagione,
Know I need first the reason,

e quinci l'indole della pozione:
and then the nature of the potion:

se calda, o frigida, se poca, o molta,
if hot, or cold, if little, or a lot,

se in una volta ovvero in più.
if at one time, or in several.
(If all at once or in several doses.)

FIORDILIGI, DORABELLA, ALFONSO
Preso han l'arsenico, signor dottore,
Taken they have the arsenic, mister doctor,

Qui dentro il bevvero,[48]
Here, inside, they drank it,

la causa è amore, ed in un sorso sel mandar giù.
the reason is love, and in one sip they gulped it down.

DESPINA
Non vi affannate, non vi turbate:
Don't get anxious, don't get upset:

Ecco una prova di mia virtù.
Here's a proof of my skill.

(Despina inizia a tirare fuori una calamita gigante dal suo sacco.)
(Despina starts to pull out a giant magnet from her sack.)

FIORDILIGI, DORABELLA, ALFONSO
Egli ha di un ferro la man fornita.
He has with an iron his hand furnished.
(He has taken up a metal object with his hand.)

DESPINA
Questo è quel pezzo di calamita pietra mesmerica,
This is the piece of magnet, stone Mesmeric,[49]

ch'ebbe l'origine nell'Alemagna,[50]
which had its origins in Germany,

che poi sì celebre là in Francia fu.
that afterwards so celebrated there in France became.

(Tocca con un pezzo di calamita la testa ai finti infermi e striscia dolcemente i loro corpi per lungo.)
(She runs the magnet over the bodies of the two men, causing them to twist, squirm and move.)

FIORDILIGI, DORABELLA, ALFONSO
Come si muovono, torcono, scuotono!
How they move, twist, shake!

In terra il cranio presto percuotono.
On (the) ground their heads soon they will hit.
(They will hit their heads on the ground any moment.)

DESPINA
Ah, lor la fronte tenete su.
Ah, their the forehead hold up.
(Hold up their foreheads.)

FIORDILIGI, DORABELLA
Eccoci pronte.
Here we are, ready.

(Sono con circospezione piazzano le loro mani sulla fronte degli uomini.)
(They gingerly place their hands on the men's foreheads.)

DESPINA
Tenete forte. Coraggio! Or liberi siete da morte.
Hold tightly. Courage! Now freed you are from death.

FIORDILIGI, DORABELLA, ALFONSO
Attorno guardano, forze riprendono…
Around them they look, strength they're regaining…

Ah, questo medico vale un Perù!
Ah, this doctor is worth a Peru![51]
(Ah, this doctor is worth his weight in gold!)

FERRANDO, GUGLIELMO
(sorgendo in piedi)
(rising)
Dove son? Che loco è questo?
Where am I? What place is this?

Chi è colui, color chi sono?
Who is he, they, who are they?

Son di Giove innanzi al trono?
Am I of Jove before the throne?
(Am I standing before Jove's throne?)

Sei tu Palla, o Citerea?
Are you Pallas or Cythera?[52]

No, tu sei l'alma mia Dea:
No, you are the soul my goddess:
(No, you are the goddess of my soul:)

Ti ravviso al dolce viso
I recognize you by (your) sweet face

e alla man ch'or ben conosco
and by the hand, that now well I know,

e che sola è il mio tesor.
and which alone is my treasure.

[53]**DESPINA, ALFONSO**
(a alle ragazze)
(to the girls)
Son effetti ancor del tosco, non abbiate alcun timor.
There are effects still of the poison, don't have any fear.

FIORDILIGI, DORABELLA
Sarà ver, ma tante smorfie fanno torto al nostro onor.
That may be true, but so many grimaces cause damage to our honor.
(That may be true, but such unseemly behavior compromises our
honor.)

FERRANDO, GUGLIELMO
(a parte)
(to themselves)
Dalla voglia ch'ho di ridere,
From the desire that I have of laughing,

il polmon mi scoppia oror.
my lung is bursting in me any moment.
(From my desire to laugh my lungs will burst at any moment!)

(alle donne)
(They now address their respective sweethearts, in reverse.)

Per pietà, bell'idol mio…
For pity's sake, lovely idol mine…

FIORDILIGI, DORABELLA
Più resister non poss'io…
No longer resist can't I…
(I can resist no longer…)

FERRANDO, GUGLIELMO
Volgi a me le luci liete.
Turn to me your eyes joyful!

DESPINA, ALFONSO
(a alle ragazze)
(to the girls)
In poch'ore lo vedrete, per virtù del magnetismo
In a few hours, you'll see, by virtue of the magnetism,

finirà quel parossismo, torneranno al primo umor.
will cease that paroxysm, they will go back to their first humor.
(their paroxysms will cease and they'll return to their normal state.)

FERRANDO, GUGLIELMO
Dammi un bacio, o mio tesoro;
Give me a kiss, my treasure;

un sol bacio o qui mi moro.
one sole kiss or here I'll die!

FIORDILIGI, DORABELLA
Stelle! Un bacio?
Heavens! A kiss?

DESPINA, ALFONSO
Secondate per effetto di bontate.
Second them, as (a) matter of goodness.
(Do as they ask, as an act of kindness.)

FIORDILIGI, DORABELLA
Ah, che troppo si richiede da una fida, onesta amante.
Ah, too much is asked from a faithful, honest lover.

Oltraggiata è la mia fede, oltraggiato è questo cor!
Outraged is my loyalty, outraged is my heart!

DESPINA, ALFONSO
(a parte)
(to themselves)
Un quadretto più giocondo
A little picture more amusing

non s'è visto in questo mondo.
hasn't been seen in all the world.

Quel che più mi fa da ridere
That which most makes me laugh

è quell'ira e quel furor.
is that anger and that fury.

FERRANDO, GUGLIELMO
Un quadretto piu giocondo
A little picure more amusing

non s'è visto in questo mondo.
hasn't been seen in all the world.

Ma non so se finta o vera
But I don't know if feigned or true

è quell'ira e quel furor.
is that anger and that fury.

FIORDILIGI, DORABELLA
Disperati, attossicati, ite al diavol quanti siete!
Desperate ones, poisoned ones, go to the devil all of you!
(You desperate, poisoned ones, go to the devil, all of you!)

tardi inver vi pentirete se più cresce il mio furor!
Later truly you'll be sorry, if more grows my fury!
(Later you'll be truly sorry if my fury increases still more!)

DESPINA, ALFONSO
Un quadretto piu giocondo non si vide in tut oil mondo, etc.

Ch'io ben so che tanto foco
For I well know that such fire

cangerassi in quel d'amor.
will change itself into that of love.
(will change into the fire of love.)

FERRANDO, GUGLIELMO
Un quadretto piu giocondo non si vide in tut oil mondo, etc.

Né vorrei che tanto fuoco terminasse in quel d'amor.
I wouldn't wish that such fire should end in that of love.
(I wouldn't wish that fire to end up as fire of love.)

FINE DI ATTO I
END OF ACT I

ATTO SECONDO
ACT II

(Una camera nella casa delle sorelle Fiordiligi, Dorabella e Despina)
(In a room in the home of Dorabella and Fiordiligi, they converse with Despina.)

DESPINA
Andate là, che siete due bizzarre ragazze!
Go on, for you're two strange girls!

FIORDILIGI
Oh, cospettaccio! Cosa pretenderesti?
Oh, good heavens! What do you want?

DESPINA
Per me, nulla.
For myself, nothing.

FIORDILIGI
Per chi, dunque?
For whom, then?

DESPINA
Per voi.
For you two.

DORABELLA
Per noi?
For us?

DESPINA
Per voi. Siete voi donne o no?
For you two. Are you women or not?

FIORDILIGI
E per questo?
What do you mean by that?

DESPINA
E per questo dovete far da donne.
I mean you must act like women.

DORABELLA
Cioè?
That is?
(How?)

DESPINA
Trattar l'amon *en bagatelle*, le occasioni belle non negliger[1] giammai;
Treat love lightly, the opportunities good not neglect ever.
(Treat love lightly and don't allow a good opportunity to slip by;)

Cangiar a tempo, a tempo esser costanti:
Change sometimes, sometimes be constant:

***coquetizzar* con grazia, prevenir la disgrazia**
flirt with charm, prevent the misfortune

sì commune a chi si fida in uomo.
so common in who trusts in a man.

Mangiar il fico e non gittar il pomo.
Eat the fig and don't throw away the apple.
(Enjoy the company of one man while keeping another one in reserve.)

FIORDILIGI
(a parte)
(to herself)
Che diavolo!
What (the) devil!

(A Despina.)
(To Despina.)

Tai cose falle tu se n'hai voglia.
Such things do them yourself if you feel like it.

DESPINA
Io già le faccio. Ma vorrei che anche voi
I already do them. But I'd like that also you

faceste un po' lo stesso. Per esempio:
did a bit (of) the same. For example:

I vostri ganimedi son andati alla guerra?
Your Ganymedes[2] have gone to war?

Infin che tornano, fate alla militare: Reclutate!
Until they return, act as soldiers do: Recruit!

DORABELLA
Il cielo ce ne guardi!
Heaven preserve us!

DESPINA
Eh, che noi siamo in terra e non in cielo!
Hey, but we are on earth and not in heaven!

Fidatevi al mio zelo.
Have faith in my eagerness (to help you).

Giacchè questi forastieri v'adorano, lasciatevi adorar.
Since these foreigners adore you, let yourselves be adored.

Son ricchi, belli, nobili, generosi,
They're rich, handsome, well born, generous,

come fede fece a voi Don Alfonso;
as assurance gave to you Don Alfonso;
(as Don Alfonso attested to you;)

Avean coraggio di morire per voi:
They had (the) courage to die for you:

Questi son merti che sprezzar non si denno
These are virtues that scorned mustn't be

da giovani qual voi belle e galanti,
by young women like you, lovely and elegant,

che pon³ star senza amor, non senza amanti.
who can be without love (but) not without lovers.

(A parte.)
(To herself.)

(Par che ci trovin gusto.)
(It seems that in this they find pleasure.)
(It seems they find the idea pleasurable.)
(I think they are catching on to the idea.)

FIORDILIGI
Per Bacco, ci faresti far delle belle cose!
By Jove, you'd have us do some lovely things!

Credi tu che vogliamo favola diventar degli oziosi?
Do you think that we want to the talk become of idlers?
(Do you think we want to become the subject of idle gossip?)

Ai nostri cari sposi credi tu che vogliam dar tal tormento?
To our dear fiancés do you think that we want to give such torment?

DESPINA
E chi dice che abbiate a far loro alcun torto?
And who says that you would have to do them any harm?

DORABELLA
Non ti par che sia torto bastante
Don't you think that it is harm enough

se noto si facesse che trattiamo costor.
if known it was that we're entertaining these (men).

DESPINA
Anche per questo c'è un mezzo sicurissimo:
Even for that there's a way most sure:

Io voglio sparger fama che vengono da me.

I want to spread (the) rumor that they're coming for me.

DORABELLA
Chi vuoi ch'il creda?

Who do you want it to believe?

(Who do you think will believe it?)

DESPINA
Oh, bella! Non ha forse merto una cameriera

Oh, come on now! Not has perhaps merit a chambermaid

d'aver due cicisbei? Di me fidatevi.

of having two admirers? Trust me.

(Come on now! Doesn't a chambermaid merit having two admirers? Trust me.)

FIORDILIGI
No. Son troppo audaci questi tuoi forastieri.

No. They're too bold, these your foreigners.

Non ebber la baldanza fin di chieder dei baci?

Didn't they have the audacity even to ask for some kisses?

DESPINA
(a parte)
(to herself)
(Che disgrazia!)
(What misfortune!)

(Alle sue amanti.)
(To her mistresses.)

Io vi posso assicurar che le cose che han fatto
I can you assure that the things that they've done

furo effetti del tossico che han preso:
were effects of the poison that they took:

Convulsioni, deliri, follie, vaneggiamenti.
Convulsions, deliriums, mad behavior, wild ravings.

Ma or vedrete come son discreti,
But now you'll see how they're discreet,

manierosi, modesti e mansueti. Lasciateli venir.
polite, modest and meek. Let them come.

DORABELLA
E poi?
And afterwards?

DESPINA
E poi? Caspita! Fate voi!
And afterwards? Blast it all! It's up to you!

(a parte)
(to herself)

(L'ho detto che cadrebbero!)
(I said that they'd fall!)

FIORDILIGI
Cosa dobbiamo far?
What must we do?

DESPINA
Quel che volete: Siete d'ossa e di carne,
Whatever you want: Are you of bone and of flesh,

o cosa siete?
or what are you?

NO. 19 ARIA

DESPINA
Una donna a quindici anni
A woman at fifteen years
(A woman at the age of fifteen)

dee saper ogni gran moda,
should know everything that goes on,

dove il diavolo ha la coda, cosa è bene, e mal cos'è;
where the devil has its tail, what is good and bad what is;
(where the devil hides its tail, what is good and what is bad;)

Dee saper le maliziette che innamorano gli amanti,
She must know the little tricks that ensnare her lovers,

finger riso, finger pianto, inventar i bei perchè.
feign laughter, feign tears, invent the good excuses.[4]

Dee in un momento dar retta a cento;
She must in one moment pay attention to a hundred (men);

colle pupille parlar con mille,
with her eyes speak with a thousand (men),

dar speme a tutti, sien belli o brutti,
give hope to all, be they handsome or ugly,

saper nascondersi senza confondersi,
know how to hide (her feelings) without becoming flustered,

senza arrossire saper mentire
without blushing know how to lie

e qual regina dall'alto soglio,
and, like a queen, from her lofty throne,

col "posso e voglio" farsi ubbidir.
with an "I can and I will" have herself obeyed.
(with an "I can and I will" command obedience.)

(a parte)
(to herself)

(Par ch'abbian gusto di tal dottrina;
(It seems that it is to their taste (of) such a doctrine;
(It appears they like my philosophy;)

Viva Despina, che sa servir.)
Long live Despina who knows how to serve.
(Long live Despina, who serves them well.)

(Parte.)
(She leaves.)

FIORDILIGI
Sorella, cosa dici?
Sister, what do you say?

DORABELLA
Io son stordita dallo spirto infernal di tal ragazza.
I am amazed by the spirit infernal of that girl.
(I am amazed at that girl's devilish audacity.)

FIORDILIGI
Ma credimi, è una pazza.
Believe me, she's a crazy one.

Ti par che siamo in caso di seguir suoi consigli?
Do you think that we can possibly (to) follow her advice?

DORABELLA
Oh certo, se tu pigli pel rovescio il negozio.
Oh, certainly, if you take upside down the business.
(Oh, certainly, if you turn the whole business upside down.)
(Certainly, if you look at the whole business from another perspective.)

FIORDILIGI
Anzi io lo piglio per il suo vero dritto;
On the contrary, I look at it from it true perspective;

Non credit tu delitto per due giovani omai promesse spose
Don't you think (it a) crime for two young at last betrothed girls

il far di queste cose?
the doing of these things?
(Don't you think it is a crime for two engaged girls like ourselves to do these things?)

DORABELLA
Ella non dice che facciamo alcun mal.
She doesn't say that we do any harm.

FIORDILIGI
È mal che basta il far parlar di noi.
It's harm enough to have them talk about us.

DORABELLA
Quando si dice che vengon per Despina!…
If we say that they're coming for Despina!…

FIORDILIGI
Oh, tu sei troppo larga di coscienza!
Oh, you are too broad of conscience!
(Oh, your conscience is too broad!)
(You're too broadminded!)

E che diranno gli sposi nostri?
And what will they say, the fiancés ours?

DORABELLA
Nulla: o non sapran l'affare, ed e tutto finito,
Nothing. Either they'll know nothing of the matter and it's all finished,

o sapran qualche cosa e allor diremo che vennero per lei.
or they'll learn something and then we'll say that they came for her.

FIORDILIGI
Ma i nostri cori?
But our hearts?

DORABELLA
Restano quel che sono. Per divertirsi un poco
They remain what they are. To amuse ourselves a little

e non morire della malinconia,
and not die of melancholy,

non si manca di fè, sorella mia.
is not lacking in faith, sister mine.

FIORDILIGI
Questo è ver.
This is true.

DORABELLA
Dunque?
Then?

FIORDILIGI
Fa' un po' tu; ma non voglio aver colpa,
Do a bit yourself; but I don't want to be blamed,

se poi nasce un imbroglio.
if afterwards arises a scandal.
(You go ahead; but I don't want to take the blame if there's a scandal afterwards.)

DORABELLA
Che imbroglio nascer deve, con tanta precauzion?
What scandal arise can, with so many precautions?
(What scandal can there be, with so many precautions?)

Per altro, ascolta: per intenderci bene,
Incidentally, listen: To understand each other well,

qual vuoi sceglier per te de' due narcisi?
which one do you wish to choose of the two Narcissi?
(which of the two Narcissi do you choose for yourself?)

FIORDILIGI
Decidi tu, sorella.
You decide, sister.

DORABELLA
Io già decisi.
I already decided.

NO. 20 DUETTO
NO. 20 DUET

DORABELLA
Prenderò quel brunettino, che più lepido mi par.
I will take that dark one, who more witty seems to me.

FIORDILIGI
Ed intanto io col biondino, vo' un po' ridere e burlar.
And meanwhile with the blond one, I'd like to a bit laugh and joke.

DORABELLA
Scherzosetta ai dolci detti io di quel risponderò.
Playfully to the sweet words I to that one will answer.
(Playfully I will answer to that one's sweet words.)

FIORDILIGI
Sospirando i sospiretti io dell'altro imiterò.
Sighing, the little sighs I of the other one will imitate.

DORABELLA
Mi dirà: "Ben mio, mi moro!"
He will say to me: "My love, I'm dying!"

FIORDILIGI
Mi dirà: "Mio bel tesoro!"
He will say to me: "My lovely treasure!"

FIORDILIGI, DORABELLA
Ed intanto che diletto, che spassetto io proverò!
And meanwhile what delight, what fun I will have!

(Don Alfonso entra.)
(Don Alfonso enters.)

ALFONSO
Ah, correte al giardino, le mie care ragazze!
Ah, run to the garden, my dear girls!

Che allegria! Che musica! Che canto!
What gaiety! What music! What singing!

Che brillante spettacolo! Che incanto! Fate presto, correte!
What brilliant display! What magic! Hurry, run!

DORABELLA
Che diamine esser può?
What the heck can it be?

ALFONSO
Tosto vedrete.
Soon you will see.

(Partono tutti. Giardino alla riva del mare. All'imbarcadero giunge una barca addobbata con fiori in cui siedono Ferrando e Guglielmo con una banda di musici. In giardino Despina, Fiordiligi, Dorabella, Don Alfonso)
(They arrive in a garden by the seashore, with grass seats and two small stone tables. By the riverbank, on a barge decorated with flowers, musicians, singers and servants congregate. Awaiting their arrival are Despina, Ferrando and Guglielmo, all richly clad.)

NO. 21 DUETTO CON CORO
NO. 21 DUET WITH CHORUS

FERRANDO, GUGLIELMO
Secondate, aurette amiche, secondate i miei desiri,
Aid, breezes friendly, my desires,
(Friendly breezes, aid my desires,)

e portate i miei sospiri alla Dea di questo cor.
and take my sighs to the goddess of this heart.

Voi che udiste mille volte il tenor[5] delle mie pene,[6]
You who heard a thousand times the strains of my woes,

ripetete al caro bene, tutto quel che udiste allor.
repeat to the dear beloved all that you heard then.

CORO
CHORUS
Secondate, aurette amiche, il desir di sì bei cor.
Aid, breezes friendly, the desire of such fine hearts.

ALFONSO
(ai servi che portano bacili con fiori)
(to the servants, who are bringing vases with flowers)
Il tutto deponete sopra quei tavolini,
Everything put down on top of those little tables,

e nella barca ritiratevi, amici.
and to the barge go back, friends.
(Put everything down on the little tables and go back to the boat,
my friends.)

DORABELLA, FIORDILIGI
Cos'è tal mascherata?
What is this masquerade?

DESPINA
(a Ferrando e Guglielmo)
(to Ferrando and Guglielmo)
Animo, via, coraggio! Avete perso l'uso della favella?
Be brave, come on, courage! Have you lost the use of words?
(Be brave, come on now, courage! Has the cat got your tongue?)

(La barca s'allontana dalla sponda.)
(The boat sails off from the riverbank.)

FERRANDO
Io tremo e palpito dalla testa alle piante.
I tremble and shake from head to foot.

GUGLIELMO
Amor lega le membra a vero amante.
Love binds the limbs of a true lover.

ALFONSO
(alle donne)
(to the women)
Da brave, incoraggiteli! (incoraggiteli!)[7]
Come on now girls, encourage them! (encourage them!)

FIORDILIGI
(agli amanti)
(to the lovers)
Parlate.
Speak.

DORABELLA
(agli amanti)
(to the lovers)
Liberi dite pur quel che bramate.
Freely tell then that which you desire.
(Tell us freely what you desire.)

FERRANDO
Madama…
My lady…

GUGLIELMO
Anzi, madame…
Rather…my ladies…

FERRANDO
Parla pur tu.
Speak also you.
(You speak.)

GUGLIELMO
No, no, parla pur tu.
No, no, you speak.

ALFONSO
Ah, cospetto del diavolo! Lasciate tali smorfie
Ah, to the devil with it all! Drop this skittishness

del secolo passato. Despinetta, terminiam questa festa:
of the century past. Despinetta, let us end this charade:
(Ah, the hell with it! Drop this old-fashioned skittishness. Despinetta, let's put an end to this charade.)

Fat u con lei quell ch'io farò con questa.
Do you with her that which I will do with this one.

NO. 22 QUARTET

ALFONSO
(prende per mano Dorabella, mentre Despina prende Fiordiligi)

(taking Dorabella by the hand; Despina takes Fiordiligi's)
La mano a me date, movetevi un po'.
Your hand to me give, move yourself a little.

(agli amanti)
(to the lovers)

Se voi non parlate per voi parlerò.
If you don't speak, for you I will speak.

(per le ragazze)
(to the girls)

Perdono vi chiede uno schiavo tremante.
Forgiveness asks of you a slave trembling.
(A trembling slave implores your pardon.)

V'offese, lo vede, ma solo un istante.
He offended you, he sees, but only for an instant.

Or pena, ma tace…
Now he suffers, but keeps silent…

FERRANDO, GUGLIELMO
Tace…
Keeps silent…

ALFONSO
Or lasciavi in pace…
Now he leaves you in peace…

FERRANDO, GUGLIELMO
In pace…
In peace…

ALFONSO
Non può quel che vuole,
He can't have what he wants,

vorrà quel che può.
he will want what he can have.

FERRANDO, GUGLIELMO
(ripetono i due versi interi con un sospiro)
(repeating Alfonso's words with a deep sigh)
Non può quel che vuole, vorrà quel che può.

ALFONSO
Su via, rispondete! Guardate…e ridete?
Come on, answer! You look…and you laugh?

DESPINA
(mettendosi davanti alle due ragazze)
(placing herself in front of the two girls)
Per voi la risposta a loro darò.
For you the answer to them I will give.
(I will answer them for you.)

Quello ch'è stato, è stato,
That which has been has been.
(What is done is done.)

Scordiamci del passato:
Let us forget about the past:

Rompasi omai quel laccio, segno di servitù.
Let it be broken henceforth that bond, symbol of servitude.
(Henceforth let this bond, a symbol of servitude, be broken.)

(Despina prende la mano di Dorabella, Don Alfonso quella di Fiordiligi; e fan rompere i lacci agli amanti, cui mettono al braccio dei medesimi.)
(Despina takes Dorabella's hand and Alfonso takes Fiordiligi's. They make them break their garlands and place them entwined around the young men's arms.)

(agli amanti)
(to the lovers)

A me porgete il braccio, né sospirate più.
To me give your arm, don't sigh any more.

ALFONSO, DESPINA
Per carità partiamo, quel che san far veggiamo.
For pity's sake let's leave, what they can do we will see.

Le stimo più del diavolo s'ora non cascan giù.
I value them more than the devil if now they don't fall down.
(I reckon the girls are smarter than the devil if they don't succumb now.)

(Despina e Don Alfonso partono. Guglielmo al braccio di Dorabella; Ferrando e Fiordiligi senza darsi braccio.)
(Dorabella takes Guglielmo's arm and Fiordiligi strolls with Ferrando. There is a bit of dumb show, with embarrassed glances and nervous laughter.)

FIORDILIGI
Oh, che bella giornata!
Oh, what a lovely day!

FERRANDO
Caldetta, anziche no.
A bit warm, than not.

DORABELLA
Che vezzosi arboscelli!
What pretty shrubs!

GUGLIELMO
Certo, son belli; han più foglie che frutti.
Certainly, they're lovely; they have more leaves than fruits.

FIORDILIGI
Quei viali come sono leggiadri. Volete passeggiar?
Those paths, how they're charming. Would you like to stroll?

FERRANDO
Son pronto, o cara, ad ogni vostro cenno.
I'm ready, oh (my) dear, for every your command.

FIORDILIGI
Troppa grazia!
You're too kind!

FERRANDO
(a Guglielmo, nel passare)
(as he passes close to Guglielmo)
Eccoci alla gran crisi!
Here we are, at the great crisis.
(Here we are, at the moment of truth.)

FIORDILIGI
Cosa gli avete detto?
What did you him tell?

FERRANDO
Eh...gli raccomandai di divertirla bene.
Er...I told him to amuse her well.

DORABELLA
(a Guglielmo)
(to Guglielmo)
Passeggiamo anche noi.
Let us stroll also (us).

GUGLIELMO
Come vi piace.
As you wish.

(Passeggiano. Dopo un momento di silenzio.)
(After a few moments of strolling.)

Ahimè!
Alas!

DORABELLA
Che cosa avete?
What is the matter with you?

GUGLIELMO
Io mi sento sì male, anima mia, che mi par di morire.
I feel so ill, my love, that I think I am dying.

DORABELLA

(a parte)

(to herself)

(Non otterrà nientissimo.)

(He won't get absolutely nothing.)

(He will get absolutely nowhere with me.)

(a Guglielmo)

(to Guglielmo)

Saranno rimasugli del velen che beveste.

It could be the residue of the poison that you drank.

GUGLIELMO

(con fuoco)

(with fire)

Ah, che un veleno assai più forte io bevo

Ah, for a poison much stronger I drink

in que' crudi e focosi mongibelli[8] amorosi!

in those cruel and fiery volcanoes amorous!

(Ah, I drink a far stronger poison from your cruel volcanoes of love!)

(Fiordiligi e Ferrando andare fuori passeggiando.)

(Fiordiligi and Ferrando go off strolling.)

DORABELLA

Sarà veleno calido; fatevi un poco fresco.

It must be poison hot; make yourself a little cool.

(It must have been some hot poison! Cool yourself down a bit.)

GUGLIELMO
Ingrata, voi burlate, ed intanto io mi moro!
Thankless one, you are joking, and meanwhile I am dying!

(A parte.)
(To himself.)

(Son spariti: dove diamin son iti?)
(They've disappeared. Where the heck have they gone?)

DORABELLA
Eh via, non fate…
Oh, go on, don't do it…
(Oh, go on, don't die…)

GUGLIELMO
Io mi moro, crudele, e voi burlate?
I am dying, cruel one, and you are joking?

DORABELLA
Io burlo?
I am joking?

GUGLIELMO
Dunque datemi qualche segno, anima bella, della vostra pietà.
Then give me some sign, soul lovely, of your pity.
(Then, my dearest, give me some sign of your pity.)

DORABELLA
Due, se volete; dite che far deggio e lo vedrete.
Two, if you wish; tell me what do I must and you'll see.

GUGLIELMO
(a parte)
(to himself)
(Scherza, o dice davvero?)
(Is she joking, or is she speaking in earnest?)

(a Dorabella, mostrandole un ciondolo)
(to Dorabella, showing her a heart-shaped locket)

Questa picciola offerta d'accettare degnatevi?
This little offering to accept will you deign?
(Would you deign to accept this little gift from me?)

DORABELLA
Un core?
A heart?

GUGLIELMO
Un core: È simbolo di quello ch'arde,
A heart. It's a symbol of that heart which burns,

languisce e spasima per voi.
languishes and suffers agonies for you.

DORABELLA
(a parte)
(to herself)
(Che dono prezioso!)
(What (a) gift precious!)

GUGLIELMO
L'accettate?
Will you accept it?

DORABELLA
Crudele! Di sedur non tentate un cor fedele.
Cruel one! To seduce don't try a heart faithful.

GUGLIELEMO
(a parte)
(to himself)
(La montagna vacilla. Mi spiace; ma impegnato
(The mountain is tottering. I don't like it, but at stake

è l'onor di soldato.)
is the honor of (a) soldier.)

(A Dorabella.)
(Aloud to Dorabella.)

V'adoro!
I adore you!

DORABELLA
Per pietà…
For pity's sake…

GUGLIELMO
Son tutto vostro!
I'm all yours!

DORABELLA
Oh, Dei!
Oh, gods!

GUGLIELMO
Cedete, o cara!
Give in, oh dearest!

DORABELLA
Mi farete morir…
You'll make me die…

GUGLIELMO
Morremo insieme, amorosa mia speme. L'accettate?
We will die together, loving my hope. Will you accept it?
(We will die together, my (beloved) loving hope. Will you accept it?)

DORABELLA
(dopo breve intervallo, con un sospiro)
(after a brief pause, with a sigh)
L'accetto!
I accept it!

GUGLIELMO
(a parte)
(to himself)
(Infelice Ferrando!)
(Unhappy Ferrando!)

(a Dorabella)
(to Dorabella)

Oh, che diletto!
Oh, what delight!

NO. 23 DUETTO
NO. 23 DUET

GUGLIELMO
Il core vi dono, bell'idolo mio.
This heart I give you, lovely idol mine.

Ma il vostro vo' anch'io: via, datelo a me.
But yours I want also I: Come, give it to me.
(But I also want yours, give it to me.)

DORABELLA
Mel date, lo prendo, ma il mio non vi rendo.
Give it to me, I'll take it, but mine I won't give you.

Invan mel chiedete: più meco ei non è.
In vain you ask me for it, no longer with me it is not.
(It's useless for you to ask for it for it's no longer mine.)

GUGLIELMO
Se teco non l'hai, perché batte qui?
If with you you don't have it, why does it beat here?

DORABELLA
Se a me tu lo dai, che mai balza lì?
If to me you give it, what ever is beating there?

DORABELLA, GUGLIELMO
È il mio coricino che più non è meco:
It is my little heart that no longer isn't with me.

Ei venne a star teco, ei batte così.
It came to be with you, it beats like that.

GUGLIELMO
(vuol metterle il cuore dove ha il ritratto di Ferrando)
(trying to put the heart where she keeps the portrait of Ferrando)
Qui lascia che il metta.
Here let that it I put in.
(Let me put it in there.)

DORABELLA
Ei qui non può star.
It here cannot stay.

GUGLIELMO
T'intendo, furbetta.
I understand you, you cunning one.

DORABELLA
Che fai?
What are you doing?

GUGLIELMO
Non guardar.
Don't look.

(Le torce dolcemente la faccia dall'altra parte, le cava il ritratto e vi mette il cuore.)
(He removes her locket with Ferrando's portrait and puts his own heart in its place.)

DORABELLA
Nel petto un Vesuvio d'avere mi par.
In my breast a Vesuvius of having it seems to me.
(I feel as if I have a Vesuvius in my breast.)

GUGLIELMO
(a parte)
(to himself)
(Ferrando meschino! Possibil non par.)
(Ferrando wretch! Possible it doesn't seem.)
(Wretched Ferrando! It doesn't seem possible.)

(a Dorabella)
(to Dorabella)

L'occhietto a me gira.
Your little eye to me turn.
(Look at me with your dear little eyes.)

DORABELLA
Che brami?
What do you want?

GUGLIELMO
Rimira se meglio può andar.
Look again if better it can go.
(Look, look, could anything be better?)

DORABELLA, GUGLIELMO
Oh, cambio felice di cori e d'affetti!
Oh, exchange happy of hearts and of affections!

Che nuovi diletti, che dolce penar!
What new delights, what sweet suffering!

(Partono abbracciati. Entrano Fiordiligi e Ferrando.)
(They go off arm in arm. Fiordiligi rushes in, followed by Ferrando.)

FERRANDO
Barbara, perché fuggi?
Cruel one, why do you run away?

FIORDILIGI
Ho visto un'aspide, un'idra, un basilisco!
I have seen a snake, a hydra, a basilisk![9]

FERRANDO
Ah crudel, ti capisco!
Ah, cruel one, I understand you!

L'aspide, l'idra, il basilisco,
The serpent, the hydra, the basilisk,

e quanto i libici deserti han di più fiero
and all that the Libyan deserts have of most ferocious

in me solo tu vedi.
in me only you see.
(and all the most ferocious beasts of the Libyan deserts is only what
you see in me.)

FIORDILIGI
È vero. Tu vuoi tormi[10] la pace.
It's true. You want to take away from me the peace of mind.
(It's true. You want to rob me of my peace of mind.)

FERRANDO
Ma per farti felice.
But to make you happy.

FIORDILIGI
Cessa di molestarmi!
Stop tormenting me!

FERRANDO
Non ti chiedo che un guardo.
I don't ask of you but one glance.

FIORDILIGI
Partiti!
Leave!

FERRANDO
Non sperarlo, se pria gli occhi men fieri a me non giri.
Don't hope for that, unless first your eyes less angry to me you
don't turn.
(Don't hope for that, unless you look on me more kindly.)

O ciel, ma tu mi guardi, e poi sospiri!
Oh heaven, but you look at me and then you sigh!

NO. 24 ARIA

FERRANDO
Ah, lo veggio: quell'anima bella
Ah, I see it. Your soul beautiful

al mio pianto resister non sa;
to my weeping resist it can't;

Non è fatta per esser rubella
She isn't made to be rebellious

agli affetti di amica pietà.
to the affections of friendly pity.
(Ah, I see it. Your sweet soul cannot resist my tears. It is not capable
of rebelling against such friendly feelings.)

In quel guardo, in quei cari sospiri
In those looks, in those dear sighs

dolce raggio lampeggia al mio cor.

sweet ray shines to my heart.

(By those glances, by those dear sighs, a sweet ray of hope lights up my heart.)

Già rispondi a miei caldi desiri,

Already you are responding to my warm desires,

già tu cedi al più tenero amor.

already you give in to the most tender love.

(Tristamente.)

(Sadly.)

Ma tu fuggi, spietata, tu taci,

But you flee, pitiless one, you are silent

ed invano mi senti languir?

and in vain you hear me languishing?

Ah, cessate, speranze fallaci:

Ah, cease, hopes false;

La crudel mi condanna a morir.

The cruel one is condemning me to die.

(Ferrando parte. Fiordiligi è lasciato solo.)

(He leaves. Fiordiligi is left alone.)

FIORDILIGI
Ei parte...Senti!...Ah, no: partir si lasci,

He's leaving...Listen!...Ah, no, leave let him,

(He's leaving...Listen!...Ah, no, let him go,)

Si tolga ai sguardi miei l'infausto oggetto
Let it be removed from the sight mine the shameful object

della mia debolezza.
of my weakness.
(Let the shameful object of my weakness be removed from my sight.)

A qual cimento il barbaro mi pose...
In what quandary that cruel man has placed me...

Un premio è questo ben dovuto a mie colpe!
A reward is this well deserved for my sins!
(This is a well-deserved reward for my sins!)

In tale istante dovea di nuovo amante
In such a moment should I of a new lover

i sospiri ascoltar?
the sighs listen to?

L'altrui querele dovea volger in gioco?
This other man's proposal should I take lightly?
(Should I at this time listen to a new lover's sighs? Should I take this other man's proposal lightly?)

Ah, questo core a ragione condanni, o giusto amore!
Ah, this heart with reason you condemn, oh righteous love!
(Oh, righteous love, you condemn my heart with good reason!)

Io ardo, e l'ardor mio non è più effetto
I am burning, and my ardor is no longer the effect

d'un amor virtuoso. È smania, affanno, rimorso,
of a love virtuous. It's craze, anxiety, remorse,

pentimento, leggerezza, perfidia e tradimento!
repentance, fickleness, perfidy and betrayal!

NO. 25 RONDO

FIORDILIGI
Per pietà, ben mio, perdona
For pity's sake, my beloved, forgive

all'error d'un'alma amante:
the transgression of a soul loving:

Fra quest'ombre e queste piante
Among these shadows and these trees

sempre ascoso, oh Dio sarà!
always hidden, oh God it shall be!

Svenerà quest'empia voglia
Will destroy this evil desire

l'ardir mio, la mia costanza, perderà la rimembranza
the boldness mine, my constancy will lose the memory

che vergogna e orror mi fa.
that shame and horror gives to me.
(My boldness will destroy this evil desire from my veins and my constancy will force me to lose the memory (of this new passion) which fills me with horror and shame.)

A chi mai mancò di fede
To who ever lacked of faith

questo vano, ingrato cor!
this vain, ungrateful heart!
(Whose fidelity did my vain, ungrateful heart betray!)

Si dovea miglior mercede,
You deserved a better reward,

caro bene, al tuo candor.
dear beloved, for your purity.

(Parte. Entrano Ferrando e Guglielmo.)
(She leaves and Ferrando and Guglielmo enter.)

FERRANDO
(molto felici)
(very happy)
Amico, abbiamo vinto!
Friend, we have won!

GUGLIELMO
Un ambo, o un terno?
A deuce or a treble.[11]

FERRANDO
Una cinquina, amico; Fiordiligi è la modestia in carne.
A quinella, (my) friend; Fiordiligi is modesty incarnate.

GUGLIELMO
Niente meno?
Nothing less?

FERRANDO
Nientissimo. Sta attento e ascolta come fu.
Absolutely nothing less. Pay attention and listen how it went.

GUGLIELMO
T'ascolto: di' pur su.
I'm listening: Tell me then.

FERRANDO
Pel giardinetto, come eravam d'accordo
In the little garden, as we had agreed

a passeggiar me metto. Le do il braccio;
to stroll I began. I give her my arm;

Si parla di mille cose indifferenti:
We talk about a thousand things trivial.

Alfine viensi all'amor.
At last we come to love.
(At last we come to the subject of love.)

GUGLIELMO
Avanti.
Go on.

FERRANDO
Fingo labbra tremanti, fingo di pianger,
I pretend lips trembling, I pretend to weep,

fingo di morir al suo piè.
I pretend to die at her feet.

GUGLIELMO
Bravo assai per mia fè. Ed ella?
Bravo indeed, by my faith! And she?

FERRANDO
Ella da prima ride, scherza, mi burla.
She at first laughs, jokes, makes fun of me.

GUGLIELMO
E poi?
And then?

FERRANDO
E poi finge d'impietosirsi.
And then she pretends to take pity on me.

GUGLIELMO
Oh, cospettaccio!
Oh, damnation!

FERRANDO
Alfin scoppia la bomba.
At last explodes the bomb.
(Finally the bombshell came.)

Pura siccome colomba al suo caro Guglielmo ella si serba:
Pure as a dove, for her dear Guglielmo she keeps herself:

Mi discaccia superba, mi maltratta, mi fugge,
She repulses me haughtily, she mistreats me, she flees from me,

testimonio rendendomi e messaggio
proof giving me and message
(giving me the message and absolute proof)

che una femmina ell'è senza paraggio.
that a woman she is without equal.

GUGLIELMO
Bravo tu, bravo io, brava la mia Penelope![12]
Bravo you, bravo me, brava my Penelope!
(Congratulations to you, me and my Penelope!)

Lascia un po' ch'io ti abbracci per sì felice augurio, o mio fido Mercurio!
Permit (a bit) that I embrace you, oh my faithful Mercury![13]
(si abbracciano)
(They embrace.)

FERRANDO
E la mia Dorabella? Come s'è diportata?
And my Dorabella? How did she behave?

Oh, non ci ho neppur dubbio!
Oh, I don't have any doubts!

Assai conosco quella sensibil alma.
Too well I know that gentle soul.

GUGLIELMO
Eppur un dubbio, parlandoti a quattr'occhi,
And yet, a doubt, speaking to you in confidence,[14]

Non saria mal se tu l'avessi.
It wouldn't be bad if you had it.
(And yet, in confidence, it wouldn't hurt if you had some doubts.)

FERRANDO
Come?
What?

GUGLIELMO
Dico così per dir.
I'm just saying that.

(A parte.)
(Aside.)

Avrei piacere d'indoragli¹⁵ la pillola.
I'd like to sweeten his pill.

FERRANDO
Stelle! Cesse ella forse alle lusinghe tue?
Stars! Gave in she perhaps to the flatteries yours?
(Heavens! Did she perhaps fall for your flattery?)

Ah, s'io potessi sospettarlo soltanto!
Ah, if I could suspect it only!
(Ah, if I so much as suspected it…)

GUGLIELMO
È sempre bene il sospettare in questo mondo.
It's always good to suspect in this world.
(It's always a good thing to be suspicious in this world.)

FERRANDO
Eterni Dei, favella! A fuoco lento non mi far qui morir…
Eternal gods, speak! At a fire slow don't make me here die…
(Eternal gods, speak to me! Don't torture me here over a slow flame!)

Ma no, tu vuoi prenderti meco spasso.
But no, you want to take for yourself with me jest.
(But no, you want to tease me.)

Ella non ama, non adora che me.

She doesn't love, doesn't adore but me.

(She doesn't love and adore anyone but me.)

GUGLIELMO
Certo! Anzi, in prova di suo amor,

Certainly! Moreover, as proof of her love,

di sua fede questo bel ritrattino ella mi diede.

of her faith, this lovely little portrait she gave to me.

(Gli mostra il ritratto che Dorabella gli ha dato.)

(He shows Ferrando the portrait Dorabella had given him.)

FERRANDO
(furioso)
(furious)
Il mio ritratto! Ah, perfida!

My portrait! Ah, wicked one!

(Vuol partire.)

(Is about to leave.)

GUGLIELMO
Ove vai?

Where are you going?

FERRANDO
A trarle il cor dal scellerato petto

To tear her heart out of (her) villainous breast

e a vendicar il mio tradito affetto.

and to avenge my betrayed affections.

GUGLIELMO
Fermati!
Stop!

FERRANDO
(risolto)
(resolved)
No, mi lascia!
No, let me go!

GUGLIELMO
Sei tu pazzo? Vuoi tu precipitarti per una donna che non val due soldi?
Are you mad? For a woman who isn't worth two cents?

(a parte)
(to himself)

(Non vorrei che facesse qualche corbelleria.)
(I wouldn't want that he do some foolishness.)
(I wouldn't want him to do something foolish.)

FERRANDO
Numi! Tante promesse, e lagrime, e sospiri,
Gods! So many promises, and tears and sighs,

e giuramenti, in sì pochi momenti come l'empia obliò?
and vows in so few moments the wicked one forgot?

GUGLIELMO
Per Bacco, io non lo so.
By Jove, I don't know.

FERRANDO
Che fare or deggio?
What to do now should I?
(What should I do now?)

A qual partito, a qual idea m'appiglio?
To what course of action, (to) what plan shall I follow?

Abbi di me pietà, dammi consiglio.
Have on me pity, give me advice.

GUGLIELMO
Amico, non saprei qual consiglio a te dar.
Friend, I wouldn't know what advice to you to give.

FERRANDO
Barbara, ingrata, in un giorno…in poche ore!…
Cruel one! Ungrateful one! In one day…in (a) few hours!…

GUGLIELMO
Certo, un caso quest'è da far stupore.
Certainly, a case this is to give astonishment.

NO. 26 ARIA

GUGLIELMO
Donne mie, la fate a tanti a tanti
Women mine, you do it to so many

che, se il ver vi deggio dir,
that, if the truth I must you tell,

se si lagnano gli amanti
if they complain, the lovers,

li comincio a compatir.

them I begin to feel sorry for.

(Dear ladies you cheat on so many men that, to tell you the truth,
if your lovers complain I begin to sympathize with them.)

Io vo' bene[16] al sesso vostro,

I am fond of the sex yours,

(I am fond of the fair sex)

lo sapete, ognun lo sa.

you know it, everyone knows it.

Ogni giorno ve lo mostro,

Every day I prove it to you,

vi do segno d'amistà;

I give you proofs of friendship;

Ma quel farla a tanti a tanti

But this doing it to so many and so many (men)

m'avvilisce in verità.

mortifies me, in truth.

Mille volte il brando presi

A thousand times my weapon I've drawn

per salvar il vostro onor,

to save your honor,

mille volte vi difesi

a thousand times I've defended you

colla bocca e più col cor;
with my mouth and even more, with my heart;

Ma quel farla a tanti a tanti

è un vizietto seccator.
is a little vice annoying.
(is an annoying little vice.)

Siete vaghe, siete amabili,
You're lovely, you're pleasant,

più tesori il ciel vi diè,
many treasures heaven has bestowed upon you,

e le grazie vi circondano
and graces surround you

dalla testa sino ai piè;
from your head down to your feet;

Ma, la fate a tanti a tanti,
But you do it to so many and so many,

che credibile non è.
that believable not it is.
(that it is unbelievable.)

Che, se gridano gli amanti,
That, if scream the lovers,

hanno certo un gran perché.[17]
they have for sure a great reason.
(If the lovers scream, they surely have good reason to.)

(Ferrando solo; poi Guglielmo e Don Alfonso.)
(He exits leaving Ferrando alone. Don Alfonso and Guglielmo sneak in later and talk in the background.)

FERRANDO
In qual fiero contrasto, in qual disordine
In what fierce conflict, in what turmoil

di pensieri e di affetti io mi ritrovo?
of thoughts and of affections I find myself again?

Tanto insolito e novo è il caso mio,
So unusual is the situation mine,

che non altri, non io basto per consigliarmi…
that no one, not (even) I myself can advise me…

Alfonso, quanto rider vorrai della mia stupidezza!
Alfonso, how laugh you will at my stupidity!

Ma mi vendicherò: saprò dal seno cancellar quell'iniqua…
But I will get revenge: I will from my breast banish that wicked woman…

Cancellarla? Troppo, oh Dio, questo cor per lei mi parla.
Banish her? Too much, oh God, this heart for her speaks to me.
(Banish her? Oh, God, my heart pleads for her too ardently.)

NO. 27 CAVATINA

FERRANDO
Tradito, schernito dal perfido cor,
Betrayed, scorned by her perfidious heart,

io sento che ancora quest'alma l'adora.

I feel that still my soul adores her.

(Even though her perfidious heart has betrayed and scorned me,
I feel that I still adore her.)

Io sento per essa le voci d'amor.

I hear for her the voices of love.

(I hear the voices of love speaking on her behalf.)

ALFONSO

(avvicinandosi a Ferrando)

(approaching Ferrando)

Bravo! Questa è costanza!

Bravo! That is fidelity!

FERRANDO

Andate, o barbaro! Per voi misero sono.

Go away, oh cruel man! Because of you miserable I am.

ALFONSO

Via, se sarete buono vi tornerò la calma antica.

Come now, if you're sensible I'll restore your peace of mind former.

Udite:

Listen:

(mostrando Guglielmo)

(He points to Guglielmo.)

Fiordiligi a Guglielmo si conserva fedel,

Fiordiligi to Guglielmo has stayed faithful,

e Dorabella infedele a voi fu.

and Dorabella unfaithful to you was.

FERRANDO
Per mia vergogna!
To my shame!

GUGLIELMO
Caro amico, bisogna far delle differenze in ogni cosa:
Dear friend, one must make distinctions in all things:

Ti pare che una sposa mancar possa a un Guglielmo?
Do you think that a fiancée betray could (to) a Guglielmo?
(Do you think a fiancée capable of betraying someone like me?)

Un picciol calcolo, non parlo per lodarmi,
A little comparison, (I'm not talking to flatter myself),

se facciamo tra noi…Tu vedi, amico,
if we make between us…You see, friend,

che un poco ho di più metro…
that a little more merit…
(I'm not talking to flatter myself, but a little comparison between
the two of us will show that I have a little more to offer…)

ALFONSO
Eh, anch'io lo dico!
Oh, also I say it.
(Oh, I agree.)

GUGLIELMO
(*a Alfonso*)
(*to Alfonso*)
Intanto mi darete cinquanta zecchinetti.
In the meanwhile you'll give me fifty little sequins.

ALFONSO
Volentieri. Pria però di pagar
Gladly. Before however paying

vo' che facciamo qualche altra esperienza.
I'd like us to make another experiment.

GUGLIELMO
Come?
What?

ALFONSO
Abbiate pazienza; infin domani siete entrambi miei schiavi:
Have patience; until tomorrow you're both my slaves:

A me voi deste parola da soldati di far quel ch'io dirò.
To me you gave word of a soldier to do what I tell you.

Venite: Io spero mostrarvi ben che folle è quel cervello
Come: I hope to show you well how foolish is the brain

che sulla frasca ancor vende l'uccello.
that on the branch still sells the bird.[18]
(Come, I hope to show you positively how foolish it is to count your
chickens before they're hatched.)

(Partono. Camera nella casa delle sorelle Despina e Dorabella.)
(They leave. Next we see a room with several doors, a mirror and a table.
Dorabella and Despina enter.)

DESPINA
Ora vedo che siete una donna di garbo.
Now I see that you are a woman of the world.

DORABELLA
Di resister tentai: quel demonietto ha un artifizio,
To resist I tried: That little demon has a cunning,

un'eloquenza, un tratto
an eloquence, some manners

che ti fa cader giù se sei di sasso.
that make you fall down even if you're of stone.
(I tried to resist him: But that little devil has such cunning, such
eloquence, such manners that he can make you succumb even if
you're made of stone.)

DESPINA
Corpo di satanasso, questo vuol dir saper!
Body of big Satan, that means knowing!
(The devil! You've really learned something!)

Tanto di raro noi povere ragazze abbiamo un po' di bene,
So rarely we poor girls have a little happiness,

che bisogna pigliarlo allor ch'ei viene.
that we have to take it when it comes.

(Entra Fiordiligi.)
(Fiordiligi enters.)

Ma ecco la sorella. Che ceffo!
But here is your sister. What a puss!

FIORDILIGI
Sciagurate! Ecco per colpa vostra in che stato mi trovo!
Wretches! Here, through your fault in what state I find myself!
(You wretches! Behold the state in which I find myself, through
your fault!)

DESPINA
Cosa è nato, cara madamigella?
What has happened, dear lady?[19]

DORABELLA
Hai qualche mal, sorella?
Do you have some illness, sister?

FIORDILIGI
Ho il diavolo, che porti me, te, lei, Don Alfonso,
I have the devil, that should take me, you, her, Don Alfonso,

i forestieri e quanti pazzi ha il mondo!
the strangers and all the madmen (that) has the world!
(I have the devil, and may he take me, you, her, Don Alfonso, the strangers and all the madmen in the world!)

DORABELLA
Hai perduto il giudizio?
Have you lost your reason?

FIORDILIGI
Peggio…Inorridisci: io amo! E l'amor mio
Worse…Be horrified…I'm in love! And my love

non è sol per Guglielmo.
isn't only for Guglielmo.

DESPINA
Meglio!
Better!
(That's better!)

DORABELLA
E che forse anche tu se' innamorata
And so it is, that also you are in love

del galante biondino?
with the gallant little blond one?
(So you have really fallen in love with the charming little blond
one?)

FIORDILIGI
(sospirando)
(sighing)
Ah, purtroppo per noi!
Ah, so much the worse for us!

DESPINA
Ma brava!
Well done!

DORABELLA
Tieni, settantamille[20] baci.
Have seventy thousand kisses.
(Here, I give you seventy thousand kisses.)

Tu il biondino, io 'l brunetto: Eccoci entrambe spose!
You the blond one, I the dark one: There! Both of us brides!

FIORDILIGI
Che dici! Non pensi agli infelici
What are you saying! Aren't you thinking of the unhappy men

che stamane partir? Aid loro pianti,
who this morning left? Of their weeping,

alla lor fedeltà tu più non pensi?
of their faithfulness you no longer don't think?

Così barbari sensi dove apprendesti?
Such cruel sentiments, where did you learn them?

Sì diversa da te come ti festi?
So unlike from yourself how did you become?
(How did you become so unlike yourself?)

DORABELLA
Odimi: sei tu certa che non muoiano in guerra,
Listen to me: Are you certain that they won't die in war,

i nostri vecchi amanti? E allora entrambe
our old lovers? And then both of us

resterem colle mani piene di mosche.
will be left with our hands full of flies.[21]

Tra un ben certo e un incerto
Between a good thing certain and an uncertain one

c'è sempre un gran divario!
there's always a big difference!
(There's always a big difference between something that is certain and something that is not!)
(A bird in hand is better than two in the bush!)

FIORDILIGI
E se poi torneranno?
And if later they should return?

DORABELLA
Se torneran, lor danno!
If they return, too bad for them!

Noi saremo allor mogli, moi saremo
We will be then wives, we will be

lontane mille miglia.
far away a thousand miles.

FIORDILIGI
Ma non so come mai
But I don't know how

si può cangiar in un sol giorno un core?
one can change in one single day a heart?

DORABELLA
Che domanda ridicola! Siam donne!
What a question ridiculous! We're women!

E poi tu, com'hai fatto?
And then you, how did you do it?

FIORDILIGI
Io saprò vincermi.
I will know how to control myself.

DESPINA
Voi non saprete nulla.
You won't know how to nothing.

FIORDILIGI
Farò che tu lo veda.
I'll make that you see it.
(I will show you.)

DORABELLA
Credi, sorella, è meglio che tu ceda.
Believe me, sister, it's better that you give in.

NO. 28 ARIA

DORABELLA
È amore un ladroncello, un serpentello è amor.
Is love a little thief, a little serpent is love.
(Love is a little thief and a little serpent.)

Ei toglie e dà la pace, come gli piace, ai cor.
He takes away and gives back the peace, as he pleases, to the hearts.

Per gli occhi al seno appena un varco aprir si fa,
Through the eyes to the bosom no sooner a path opened has he,
(No sooner has he opened a path through your eyes to your heart,)

che l'anima incatena e toglie libertà.
than the soul he enchains and takes away freedom.
(than he takes away your freedom and enchains your soul.)

Porta dolcezza e gusto se tu lo lasci far;
He brings sweetness and pleasure if you let him have his way;

Ma t'empie di disgusto se tenti di pugnar.
But he fills you with loathing if you try to fight (him back.)

Se nel tuo petto ei siede, s'egli ti becca qui,
If in your breast he settles, if he pecks at you here,
(If he settles in your heart, and if he has bitten you here,)

fa tutto quel ch'ei chiede che anch'io farò così.
do everything that he asks, for also I will do thus.
(do everything that he asks, as I shall do too.)

(Dorabella e Despina partono.)
(Dorabella and Despina leave.)

FIORDILIGI
Come tutto congiura a sedurre il mio cor!
How everything conspires to tempt my heart!

Ma no! Si mora e non si ceda!
But no! I'd (rather) die and I won't give in!
(But no! I'd rather die than yield!)

Errai quando alla suora
I was wrong when to my sister

io mi scopersi ed alla serva mia:
I revealed myself and to the servant mine.
(I was wrong to reveal my feelings to my sister and my servant.)

Esse a lui diran tutto, ed ei, più audace,
They to him will tell everything, and he, more bold,

fia di tutto capace...
will be of everything capable...
(Those two will tell him everything; that will embolden him and he is capable of doing anything...)

Agli occhi miei mai più non comparisca!
To my eyes never again should he present himself!
(May he never appear before my eyes again!)

A tutti i servi minaccerò il congedo,
To all the servants I will threaten the dismissal,

(Ferrando, Guglielmo e Don Alfonso ascoltando della porta, non veduti da Fiordiligi.)
(Ferrando, Guglielmo and Alfonso come in and overhear the last portion of Fiordiligi's speech.)

se lo lascian passar; veder non voglio quel seduttor.
if they let him come in; to see I don't wish that seducer.
(I will threaten all the servants with dismissal if they let him in. I don't wish to see that seducer.)

GUGLIELMO
(agli amici)
(to his friends)
Bravissima, la mia casta Artemisia! La sentite!
Well said, my chaste Artemis![22] Do you hear her!

FIORDILIGI
Ma potria Dorabella senza saputa mia…
But could Dorabella without knowledge mine…

Piano…un pensiero per la mente mi passa:
Wait…a thought through my mind is passing:
(Wait…I've just had an idea:)

In casa mia restar molte uniformi
In house mine remained many uniforms

di Guglielmo e Ferrando...
of Guglielmo and of Ferrando...

Ardir...Despina!
Be daring...Despina!

(Despina entrando.)
(Despina enters.)

DESPINA
Cosa c'è?
What is it?

FIORDILIGI
Tieni un po' questa chiave, e senza replica,
Take for a moment this key and without argument,

senza replica alcuna,
without any argument at all,

prendi nel guardaroba, e qui mi porta
take from the wardrobe and here bring me

due spade, due cappelli,
two swords, two hats,

e due vestiti de' nostri sposi.
and two uniforms belonging to our fiancés.

DESPINA
E che volete fare?
And what do you want to do?

FIORDILIGI
Vanne; non replicare.
Go! Don't ask questions.

DESPINA
(Commanda in *abrégé* donna Arroganza!)
(Commands in short[23] Miss Arrogance!)
(What shortness in her orders, Miss Arrogance!)

(Despina parte.)
(She leaves.)

FIORDILIGI
Non c'è altro: ho speranza che Dorabella
There's nothing else to do: I have hope that Dorabella

stessa seguirà l'esempio. Al campo!
herself will follow my example. To the battlefield!

Altra strada non resta per serbarci innocenti.
Another way doesn't remain to keep ourselves pure.

ALFONSO
(a parte)
(to himself)
Ho capito abbastanza.
I've understood enough.
(I've heard and understood what she's up to.)

(Per Despina, coloro che entra con le divise.)
(To Despina, who enters with the uniforms.)

Vanne pur, non temer.
Go then, don't fear.
(Go to her, don't fear.)

DESPINA
(a Fiordiligi)
(to Fiordiligi)
Eccomi.
Here I am.

FIORDILIGI
Vanne. Sei cavalli di posta voli un servo a ordinar.
Go. Six horses of post hurry a servant to order.
(Go and arrange for a servant to hurry and get six post horses.)

Di' a Dorabella che parlar le vorrei.
Tell Dorabella that speak with her I would like.

DESPINA
Sarà servita.
It shall be done.

(A parte.)
(To herself.)

(Questa donna mi par di senno uscita.)
(This woman seems to me of senses left.)
(This woman seems to be out of her mind.)

(Lei lascia.)
(She leaves.)

FIORDILIGI
L'abito di Ferrando sarà buono per me;
The suit of Ferrando will be good for me;
(Ferrando's uniform will fit me;)

Può Dorabella prender quel di Guglielmo.
Can Dorabella take the one of Guglielmo.
(Dorabella can take Guglielmo's.)

In questi arnesi raggiungerem gli sposi nostri:
In this guise we'll rejoin the fiancés ours:
(In this guise we'll rejoin our fiancés:)

Al loro fianco pugnar potremo,
By their side fight we can,

e morir, se fa d'uopo.
and die, if necessary.

(Si toglie il velo.)
(She removes her headdress.)

Ite in malora, ornamenti fatali! Io vi detesto.
Go to the devil, ornaments accursed! I detest you.

GUGLIELMO
(agli amici)
(to his friends)
(Si può dar un amor simile a questo?)
(Can there be a love similar to this one?)

FIORDILIGI
Di tornar non sperate alla mia fronte
Of returning do not hope to my brow
(Do not hope to be worn on my brow again)

pria ch'io qui torni col mio ben;
before that I here return with my beloved;

Frank Lopardo as Ferrando, 1991
METROPOLITAN OPERA ARCHIVES

Cecilia Bartoli as Despina, 1996
METROPOLITAN OPERA ARCHIVES

Renée Fleming as Fiordiligi, 1996
METROPOLITAN OPERA ARCHIVES

Thomas Allen as Don Alfonso, 2005
MARTY SOHL/METROPOLITAN OPERA

Barbara Frittoli as Fiordiligi and Nuccia Focile as Despina, 2005
MARTY SOHL/METROPOLITAN OPERA

Magdalena Kožená as Dorabella, 2005
Marty Sohl/Metropolitan Opera

Thomas Allen as Don Alfonso, Matthew Polenzani as Ferrando, and Mariusz Kwiecien as Guglielmo, 2005
MARTY SOHL/METROPOLITAN OPERA

Nathan Gunn as Guglielmo, Danielle de Niese as Despina, and Pavol Breslik as Ferrando, 2010
MARTY SOHL/METROPOLITAN OPERA

Isabel Leonard as Dorabella and Miah Persson as Fiordiligi, 2010

Susanna Phillips as Fiordiligi, 2013

In vostro loco porrò questo cappello.
In your stead I will put on this hat.

Oh, come ei mi trasforma le sembianze e il viso!
Oh, how it transforms me the appearance and the face!

Come appena io medesma or mi ravviso!
How barely I myself recognize myself!

NO. 29 DUETTO, FIORDILIGI, FERRANDO
NO. 29 DUET, FIORDILIGI, FERRANDO

FIORDILIGI
Tra gli amplessi in pochi istanti
In the embraces in a few moments

giungerò del fido sposo
I will be of the faithful betrothed.
(I will soon be in the arms of my faithful betrothed.)

Sconosciuta a lui davanti in quest'abito verrò.
Unbeknownst to him before in this attire I will come.
(I will come before him without his knowledge.)

Oh che gioia il suo bel core proverà nel ravvisarmi!
Oh, what joy his lovely heart will feel at recognizing me!

FERRANDO
(entrando)
(entering, to Fiordiligi)
Ed intanto di dolore, meschinello io mi morrò.
And meanwhile of grief, wretched I will die.

FIORDILIGI
Cosa veggio! Son tradita. Deh, partite!
What do I see! I'm betrayed. Please, leave!

FERRANDO
(prende la spada dal tavolino)
(taking the sword off the table and unsheathing it)
Ah, no, mia vita! con quel ferro di tua mano
Ah, no, my life! With that sword by your hand

questo cor tu ferirai;
this heart you will pierce;

E se forza non hai,
And if strength you don't have,

io la man ti reggerò.
I your hand will guide.

(Si inginocchia.)
(He kneels.)

FIORDILIGI
Taci, ahimè! Son abbastanza tormentata ed infelice!
Be silent, alas! I am sufficiently tormented and unhappy!

FERRANDO, FIORDILIGI
Ah che omai la sua (la mia) costanza
Ah that now her (my) constancy

a quei sguardi, a quel che dice
at those glances, at what he/she says

comincia a vacillar.
begins to waver.

FIORDILIGI
Sorgi!
Rise!

FERRANDO
Invan lo credi.
In vain you believe it.
(It's useless to insist.)

FIORDILIGI
Per pietà, da me che chiedi?
For pity's sake, from me what do you want?

FERRANDO
Il tuo cor, o la mia morte.
Your heart or my death.

FIORDILIGI
Ah, non son, più forte…
Ah, I am not any longer strong…

FERRANDO
Cedi, cara!
Yield, dearest!

(Le prende la mano e gliela bacia.)
(He takes her hand and kisses it.)

FIORDILIGI
Dei, consiglio!
Gods, advice!
(Advise me, gods!)

FERRANDO
Volgi a me pietoso il ciglio:
Turn to me pitying your eyes:

In me sol trovar tu puoi
In me only find you can

sposo, amante…e più se vuoi.
husband, lover…and more if you wish.

(tenerissimamente)
(Most tenderly.)

Idol mio, più non tardar.
Idol mine, more do not delay.

FIORDILIGI
(tremando)
(trembling)
Giusto ciel! Crudel, hai vinto:
Merciful heaven! Cruel man, you've won:

Fa di me quel che ti par.
Do with me what you want.

FIORDILIGI, FERRANDO
Abbracciamci o caro bene,
Let us embrace oh dearest beloved,

e un conforto a tante pene
and a comfort for so much suffering

sia languir di dolce affetto,
be it to languish with sweet affection

di diletto sospirar.
of delight to sigh.
(and let a comfort for all our suffering be to languish with sweet affection and to sigh with delight.)

(Partono. Don Alfonso e Guglielmo entrano.)
(They exit and Guglielmo and Alfonso enter.)

GUGLIELMO
Ah, poveretto me! Cosa ho veduto, cosa ho sentito mai!
Ah, poor me! What have I seen, what have I heard!

ALFONSO
Per carità, silenzio!
For pity's sake, silence!

GUGLIELMO
Mi pelerei la barba, mi graffierei la pelle,
I'll pull out my beard, I'll tear out my skin,

e darei colle corna entro le stelle!
and I'll butt with my horns against the stars!
(and I'll butt the stars with my cuckold's horns!)

Fu quella Fiordiligi, la Penelope, l'Artemisia del secolo!
It was she, Fiordiligi, my Penelope, the Artemis of the century!

Briccona, assassina, furfante, ladra, cagna!
Rascal, murderess, scoundrel, thief, bitch!

ALFONSO
(lieto, fra sé)
(happily, to himself)
Lasciamolo sfogar.
Let's let him blow off steam.

FERRANDO
(entrando)
(entering)
Ebben?
Well?

GUGLIELMO
La mia Fior…fior di diavolo,
My Fior…flower of (the) devil,[24]

che strozzi lei prima e dopo me!
may he choke her first and then me!

FERRANDO
(ironicamente)
(ironically)
Tu vedi bene: V'han delle differenze in ogni cosa.
You see well: There are some differences in everything.

Un poco di più merto…
A little more to offer…

GUGLIELMO
Ah, cessa, cessa di tormentarmi; ed una via piuttosto
Ah, cease tormenting me; and a way rather

studiam di castigarle sonoramente.
let us study to punish (them) soundly.

ALFONSO
Io so qual è: sposarle.
I know what it is: marry them.

GUGLIELMO
Vorrei piuttosto sposare la barca di Caronte.
I'd rather marry the ferry of Charon.[25]

FERRANDO
La grotta di Vulcano.
The grotto of Vulcan.[26]

GUGLIELMO
La porta dell'inferno.
The door of hell.

ALFONSO
Dunque restate celibi in eterno.
Then stay bachelors for all eternity.

FERRANDO
Mancheran forse donne ad uomini come noi?
Will there lack maybe women for men like us?

ALFONSO
Non c'è abbondanza d'altro.
There isn't abundance of anything else.
(There are plenty of women.)

Ma l'altre che faran se ciò fer queste?
But the others what will they do if this did these?
(But if these women did this, what will the others do?)

In fondo voi le amate
Down deep you love them

queste vostre cornacchie spennacchiate.
these, your crows plucked.
(down deep you love these plucked crows of yours.)

GUGLIELMO
Ah, purtroppo!
Ah, indeed!

FERRANDO
Purtroppo!
Indeed!

ALFONSO
Ebben, pigliatele com'elle son. Natura non potea
Well then, take them as they are. Nature couldn't

fare l'eccezione, il privilegio
make exception, the privilege

di creare due donne d'altra pasta,
of creating two women of different stuff

per i vostri bei musi. In ogni cosa
for your pretty mugs. In every thing

ci vuol filosofia. Venite meco:
you need philosophy. Come with me.

Di combinar le cose studierem la maniera.
Of arranging the matter we will study the way.
(We will find a way to arrange matters.)

Vo' che ancor questa sera
I want that still this evening

doppie nozze si facciano.
double weddings should be performed.

Frattanto, un'ottava ascoltate:
In the meantime, an octave[27] listen to:

Felicissimi voi, se la imparate.
Very happy you, if you learn it.
(In the meantime listen to this poem. If you learn it by heart, you
will be very happy.)

NO. 30 ANDANTE

ALFONSO
Tutti accusan le donne ed io le scuso,
Everyone accuses the women, and I excuse them

se mille volte al dì cangiano amore.
if a thousand times a day they change (their) love.

Altri un vizio lo chiama ed altri un uso:
Some a vice call it and others a habit:

Ed a me par necessità del core.
And to me it seems (a) necessity of the heart.

L'amante che si trova alfin deluso
The lover who finds himself in the end deceived

non condanni l'altrui, ma il proprio errore;
let him not condemn the other one's but his own mistake;
(should blame no other than himself;)

Giàcche giovani, vecchie, e belle e brutte,
Since young ones, old ones and lovely ones and ugly ones,

ripetete con me: "Così fan tutte!"
repeat with me: "Thus behave all women!"
(repeat with me: "All women behave like that!")

FERRANDO, GUGLIELMO, ALFONSO
Così fan tutte!

(Despina entra.)
(Despina enters.)

DESPINA
Vittoria, padroncini! A sposarvi disposte
Victory, dear masters! To marry you ready

son le care madame.
are the dear ladies.

A nome vostro loro io promisi che in tre giorni
In the name yours them I promised that in three days

circa partiranno con voi.
more or less they will leave with you.

L'ordin mi diero di trovar un notaio
The order they gave me to find a notary

che stipuli il contratto; alla lor camera
to draw up the (marriage) contract; in their room

attendendo vi stanno. Siete così contenti?
waiting for you they are. Are you then pleased?

FERRANDO, GUGLIELMO, ALFONSO
Contentissimi.
Very satisfied.

DESPINA
Non è mai senza effetto,
It never fails to get result,

Quand'entra la Despina in un progetto.
When enters Despina in a project.
(When Despina has a hand in a project.)

NO. 31 FINALE

(Una sala illuminata a festa. Una tavola apparecchiata per quattro.
Despina e le serve stanno facendo i preparativi per le nozze.)
(In a magnificently illuminated room with an orchestra in the background, a
table with silver candlesticks is set for four people. Despina is giving orders
and is surrounded by servants and musicians.)

DESPINA
Fate presto o cari amici
Hurry up oh dear friends

alle faci il foco date
to the torches the fire give
(light the torhces)

e la mensa preparate
and the table prepare

con ricchezza e nobiltà.
with richness and nobility.

Delle nostre padroncine gl'imenei son già disposti.
Of our mistresses the marriages are already arranged.

(ai suonatori)
(to the musicians)

E voi gite ai vostri posti finché i sposi vengon qua.
And you go to your places until the bridegrooms come here.

CORO DEI DIPENDENTI E MUSICISTI
CHORUS OF SERVANTS AND MUSICIANS
Facciam presto, o cari amici,
Let's hurry up, oh dear friends,

Alle faci il foco diamo.
To the torches the fire let us give.
(Let us light the torches.)

E la mensa prepariamo
And the table let us prepare

con ricchezza e nobiltà.
with richness and nobility.

ALFONSO
Bravi! Ottimamente! Che abbondanza! Che eleganza!
Well done! Excellent! What abundance! What elegance!

Una mancia conveniente l'un e l'altro a voi darà.
A tip suitable one and the other to you will give.
(Both gentlemen will give you suitable tips.)

(Mentre Don Alfonso canta, i suonatori accordano.)
(While Alfonso is singing the musicians tune their instruments.)

Le due coppie omai s'avanzano.
The two couples now are coming forward.

Fate plauso al loro arrivo:
Make applause at their arrival:

Lieto canto e suon giulivo
(May) happy singing and sound joyful

empia il ciel d'ilarità.
fill heaven with gaiety.

DESPINA, ALFONSO
(piano, partendo per diverse porte)
(softly, as they go off by different doors)
La più bella commediola
The most beautiful little comedy

non s'è vista o si vedrà!
hasn't been seen or will be seen!
(A finer little comedy was never seen nor ever shall be.)

(Entrano Fiordiligi, Dorabella, Ferrando e Guglielmo.)
(As the couples enter the orchestra plays a march and the chorus sings.)

CORO
CHORUS
Benedetti i doppi coniugi
Blessed be the two bridegrooms

e le amabili sposine!
and the charming brides!

Splenda lor il ciel benefico,
Let it shine on them heaven benevolently,

ed a guisa di galline
and in the manner of chickens

sien di figli ognor prolifiche
may they be of children always prolific

che le agguaglino in beltà.
that should equal them in beauty.
(And in the manner of chickens, may they produce an abundance
of children who will be as beautiful as they are.)

FIORDILIGI, DORABELLA, FERRANDO, GUGLIELMO
Come par che qui prometta
How it seems that here promises

tutto gioia e tutto amore!
everything joy and all love!
(How everything seems to promise so much love and joy!)

Della cara Despinetta certo il merito sarà.
Of dear Despinetta certainly the merit it shall be.

Raddoppiate il lieto suono, replicate il dolce canto,
Redouble your happy tunes, repeat the happy song,

e noi qui seggiamo intanto in maggior giovialità.
and we here let us sit meanwhile in greater enjoyment.
(Play your happy tunes again, repeat your happy songs and meanwhile we will sit here and enjoy ourselves.)

CORO
CHORUS
Benedetti i doppi coniugi, etc.

FERRANDO, GUGLIELMO
Tutto o vita mia al mio fuocco or ben risponde.
Everything, oh life mine, to my ardor now well responds.
(My love, everything fulfills my desires.)

FIORDILIGI, DORABELLA
Pel mio sangue l'allegria cresce e si diffonde.
Through my blood happiness grows and spreads.

FERRANDO, GUGLIELMO
Sei pur bella!
You're so lovely!

FIORDILIGI, DORABELLA
Sei pur vago!
You're so handsome!

FERRANDO, GUGLIELMO
Che bei rai!
What lovely eyes!

FIORDILIGI, DORABELLA
Che bella bocca!
What lovely mouth!

FERRANDO, GUGLIELMO
Tocca e bevi! Bevi e tocca!
Clink and drink! Drink and clink!

FIORDILIGI, DORABELLA, FERRANDO
E nel tuo, nel mio bicchiero
And in yours, in my glass

si sommerga ogni pensiero,
let it be drowned every thought,

e non resti più memoria
and let there not remain any longer a memory

del passato ai nostri cor.
of the past in our hearts.

GUGLIELMO
(piano, a parte)
(softly, aside)
(Ah, bevessero del tossico, queste volpi senza onor!)
(Ah, if they only would drink poison, these vixens without honor!)

(Entra Don Alfonso. Entra Despina travestita da notaio.)
(Alfonso enters with Despina disguised as a notary.)

ALFONSO
Miei Signori, tutto è fatto:
Ladies and gentlemen, all is ready:

Col contratto nuziale
With the contract nuptial

il notaio è sulle scale,
the notary is on the steps,

e ipso fatto qui verrà.
and very soon here will be.
(The notary is coming up the steps with the marriage contract and will be here in a moment.)

FIORDILIGI, DORABELLA, FERRANDO, GUGLIELMO
Bravo, bravo! Passi subito!
Bravo, bravo! Send him in at once!
ALFONSO
Vo' a chiamarlo: Eccolo qua.
I'm going to call him: Here he is.

DESPINA
(con voce nasale)
(in a nasal voice)[28]
Augurandovi ogni bene,
Wishing you every blessing,

il notaio Beccavivi coll'usata a voi sen viene notariale dignità.
the notary Beccavivi with his usual to you comes notarial dignity.
(Notary Beccavivi comes to you with his usual notarial dignity.)

E il contratto stipulato colle regole ordinarie
And the contract stipulated with rules prescribed

nelle forme giudiziarie, pria tossendo, poi sedendo,
in the formulations judiciary, first coughing, then sitting
(And the stipulated contract with its prescribed rules in the legal formulations, first coughing, then sitting.)

clara **voce leggerà.**
(in a) clear voice he will read.

FIORDILIGI, DORABELLA, FERRANDO, GUGLIELMO, ALFONSO
Bravo, in verità!
Well done, in truth!

DESPINA
Per contratto da me fatto
By (the) contract by me drawn up

si congiunge in matrimonio
are united in matrimony

Fiordiligi con Sempronio,
Fiordiligi with Sempronio,

e con Tizio, Dorabella,
and with Tizio, Dorabella,

sua legittima sorella:
her legitimate sister:

quelle, dame Ferraresi; questi, nobili albanesi.
those ladies from Ferrara; these noble Albanians.[29]

FIORDILIGI, DORABELLA, FERRANDO, GUGLIELMO
Cose note! Vi crediamo, ci fidiamo,
Things known! We believe you! We trust you,
(We know all that!)

soscriviam: date pur qua.
we will sign. Give it here.

DESPINA, ALFONSO
Bravi, in verità!
Well done, in truth!

(La carta resta in mano di Don Alfonso. Si sente un gran suono di tamburo.)
(The paper stays in Alfonso's hand. A loud drum roll is heard and a far-away song.)

CORO
CHORUS
(interno)
(off stage)
Bella vita militar, etc.

FIORDILIGI, DORABELLA, FERRANDO, GUGLIELMO
Che rumor, che canto è questo?
What noise, what song is this?

ALFONSO
State cheti; vo' a guardar.
Be quiet; I'm going to look.

(Va alla finestra.)
(He goes to the window.)

Misericordia! Numi del cielo!
Mercy on us! Gods in heaven!

Che caso orribile! Io tremo! Io gelo!
What situation horrible! I tremble! I freeze!

Gli sposi vostri…
The fiancés yours…

FIORDILIGI, DORABELLA
Lo sposo mio…
The fiancé mine…

ALFONSO
In questo istante tornaro, oh Dio;
In this instant they've returned, oh God;

ed alla riva sbarcano già!
and on the shore they are disembarking already!

FIORDILIGI, DORABELLA, FERRANDO, GUGLIELMO
Cosa mai sento! Barbare stelle!
What do I hear! Cruel stars!

In tal momento che si farà?
In such a moment what can be done?

(I servi portano via la tavola, e i suonatori partono in fretta.)
(The servants remove the table and the musicians escape in haste.)

FIORDILIGI, DORABELLA
(agli amanti)
(to the lovers)
Presto, partite!
Quickly, leave!

DESPINA, ALFONSO   **FERRANDO, GUGLIELMO**
Ma se li veggono?   **(ci veggono?)**
But if they see them?   (they see us?)

FIORDILIGI, DORABELLA
Presto fuggite!
Quickly, run away!

DESPINA, ALFONSO	**FERRANDO, GUGLIELMO**
Ma se li incontrano?	**(ci incontrano?)**
But if they meet them?	(meet us?)

(Don Alfonso conduce Despina in una camera.)
(Don Alfonso hides Despina.)

FIORDILIGI, DORABELLA
Là, là, celatevi, per carità.
There, there, hide yourselves, for pity's sake.

(Fiordiligi e Dorabella conducono gli amanti in un'altra. Gli amanti
escono non veduti e partono.)
(They take the men into another room where they exit unseen.)

Numi, soccorso!
Gods, help!

ALFONSO
Rasserenatevi…
Calm yourselves…

FIORDILIGI, DORABELLA
Numi, consiglio!
Gods, advice!

ALFONSO
Ritranquillatevi…
Get hold of yourselves…

FIORDILIGI, DORABELLA
(quasi frenetiche)
(almost frenetic)
Chi dal periglio ci salverà?
Who from this peril will save us?

ALFONSO
In me fidatevi: ben tutto andrà.
In me put your trust: Well everything will go.

FIORDILIGI, DORABELLA
Mille barbari pensieri
A thousand cruel thoughts

tormentando il cor mi vanno:
tormenting my heart are:

Se discoprono l'inganno,
If they discover the deceit,

ah, di noi che mai sarà!
ah, to us what will happen!

(Ferrando e Guglielmo entrano, non più travestiti.)
(Ferrando and Guglielmo appear in their military outfits.)

FERRANDO, GUGLIELMO
Sani e salvi agli amplessi amorosi
Sound and safe, to the embraces loving

delle nostre fidissime amanti,
of our most faithful sweethearts
(Safe and sound we return to our most faithful sweethearts' embraces.)

ritorniamo di gioia esultanti
we return with joy exulting

per dar premio alla lor fedeltà.
to give reward to their faithfulness.
(We return in joyful exultation to reward their faithfulness.)

ALFONSO
Giusti Numi! Guglielmo, Ferrando!
Merciful gods! Guglielmo, Ferrando!

O che giubilo! Qui? Come? Quando?
Oh, what jubilation! Here? How? When?

FERRANDO, GUGLIELMO
Richiamati da regio contrordine,
Recalled by (a) royal countermand,

pieno il cor di contento e di gaudio,
full our heart with happiness and with celebration,

ritorniamo alle spose adorabili,
we return to our fiancées adorable,

ritorniamo alla vostra amistà.
we return to your friendship.

GUGLIELMO
(a Fiordiligi)
(to Fiordiligi)
Ma cos'è quel pallor, quel silenzio?
But what is that pallor, that silence?

FERRANDO
(a Dorabella)
(to Dorabella)
L'idol mio perché mesto si sta?
My beloved why sad are you?

ALFONSO
Dal diletto, confuse ed attonite,
From delight confused and overcome

mute si restano là.
speechless they stay over there.

FIORDILIGI, DORABELLA
(a parte)
(to themselves)
(Ah che al labbro le voci mi mancano,
(Ah, (that) my lips, my voice are failing me,

se non moro un prodigio sarà.)
if I don't die a miracle it will be.)

(I servi portano un baule.)
(The servants bring in a trunk.)

GUGLIELMO
Permettete che sia posto quel baul in quella stanza…
Permit that it be put that trunk in that room…

(Esce dalla porta per la quale è uscita Despina, e rientra immediatamente.)
(He leaves by the door through which Despina had exited and re-enters immediately.)

Dei, che veggio! Un uom nascosto?
Gods, what do I see! A man in hiding?

Un notaio! Qui che fa?
A notary! Here what is he doing?

DESPINA
(rientrando, ma senza cappello)
(entering, without her hat)
No, signor, non è un notaio:
No, sir, it isn't a notary:

È Despina mascherata che dal ballo or è tornata
It's Despina in disguise who from the ball now has returned

e a spogliar si venne qua.
and to undress now has come here.

(A parte.)
(To herself.)

(Una furba che m'agguagli dove mai si troverà?)
(A clever girl that can compare to me where ever can she be found?)

FERRANDO, GUGLIELMO
(a parte)
(to themselves)
(Una furba che uguale a questa dove mai si troverà?)
(A clever girl like this one where ever can she be found?)

(Don Alfonso lascia cadere accortamente il contratto sottoscritto dalle donne.)
(Alfonso cunningly lets fall the marriage contract signed by the women.)

FIORDILIGI, DORABELLA
La Despina! Non capisco come va.
Despina! I don't understand what's going on.

ALFONSO
(piano, agli amanti)
(softly, to the men)
Già cader lasciai le carte. Raccoglietele con arte.
Already fall I let the papers. Pick them up with dissimulation.

FERRANDO
(raccoglie il contratto)
(picking up the contract)
Ma che carte sono queste?
But what papers are these?

GUGLIELMO
Un contratto nuziale?
A contract nuptial?
(A wedding contract?)

FERRANDO, GUGLIELMO
Giusto ciel! Voi qui scriveste;
Merciful heaven! You here wrote;

Contraddirci omai non vale!
To deny it to us now it's no use!

Tradimento! Ah, si faccia il scoprimento,
Betrayal! Ah, let's make the uncovering,
(Betrayal! Ah, let's uncover the truth,)

e a torrenti, a fiumi, a mari
and in torrents, in rivers, in seas

indi il sangue scorrerà.
then the blood will flow.

(Vanno per entrare nell'altra camera; le donne li arrestano.)
(They begin to go into the other room but the women stop them.)

FIORDILIGI, DORABELLA
Ah, signor, son rea di morte,
Ah, sir, I am guilty of mortal sin,

e la morte io sol vi chiedo.
and death I alone ask you for.

Il mio fallo tardi vedo:
My crime too late I see:

Con quel ferro un sen ferrite
With that sword a breast pierce

che non merita pietà.
that doesn't deserve pity.

FERRANDO, GUGLIELMO
Cosa fu?
What was it?

FIORDILIGI
(additando Despina e Don Alfonso)
(pointing to Alfonso and Despina)
Per noi favelli il crudel, la seduttrice...
For us let him speak, that cruel man, that temptress...

ALFONSO
Troppo vero è quel che dice,
Too true is that what she says,

e la prova è chiusa lì.
and the proof is shut in there.

(Accenna la camera dov'erano entrati prima gli amanti. Ferrando e Guglielmo entrano in camera.)
(He points to the room where the men had entered at first. Ferrando and Guglielmo go inside.)

FIORDILIGI, DORABELLA
Dal timor io gelo, io palpito:
From fear I freeze and tremble:

perché mai li discoprì!
why ever did he give them away!

(Ferrando e Guglielmo escono dalla camera, senza cappelli, senza mantelli e senza mustacchi, ma coll'abito finto e burlano in modo ridicolo le amanti e Despina.)
(Ferrando and Guglielmo come out of the room without hat and cloak and without mustaches, but with their fake costumes; they mock in a ridiculous fashion their Albanian other selves.)

FERRANDO
(facendo inchini esagerati a Fiordiligi)
(making exaggerated gestures to Fiordiligi)
A voi s'inchina, bella damina,
To you bows, beautiful little lady,

il cavaliere dell'Albania!
the gentleman from Albania!

GUGLIELMO
(a Dorabella)
(to Dorabella, giving the portrait back to her)
Il ritrattino pel coricino,
The little portrait for the little heart,

ecco io le rendo, signora mia.
here, I give it back to you, lady mine.

FERRANDO, GUGLIELMO
(a Despina)
(to Despina)
Ed al magnetico signor dottore
And to the magnetic mister doctor

rendo l'onore che meritò.
I give the honor that he deserved.

FIORDILIGI, DORABELLA, DESPINA
Stelle! Che veggo!
Stars! What do I see!

FERRANDO, GUGLIELMO, ALFONSO
Son stupefatte!
They're stupefied!

FIORDILIGI, DORABELLA, DESPINA
Al duol non reggo!
At grief I cannot bear it!
(I cannot bear such grief!)

FERRANDO, GUGLIELMO, ALFONSO
Son mezze matte!
They're half crazed!

FIORDILIGI, DORABELLA
(accennando Don Alfonso)
(pointing to Alfonso)
Ecco là il barbaro che c'ingannò!
There is the cruel man who deceived us!

ALFONSO
V'ingannai, ma fu l'inganno
I deceived you, but was the deception

disinganno ai vostri amanti
undeception to your lovers,
(I deceived you, but the deception was to undeceive your lovers,)

che più saggi omai saranno,
who more wise now will be,

che faran quel ch'io vorrò.
who will do that which I want.
(who will be wiser now and will do whatever I wish.)

(Li unisce e li fa abbracciare.)
(He joins them and makes them embrace.)

Qua le destre: siete sposi.
Here the right hands: you're betrothed.
(Join hands.)

Abbracciatevi e tacete.
Embrace and keep quiet.

Tutti quattro ora ridete,
All four now laugh,

ch'io già risi e riderò.
for I already have laughed and will laugh (again).

FIORDILIGI, DORABELLA
Idol mio, se questo è vero,
My beloved, if this is true,

colla fede e coll'amore
with my fidelity and my love

compensar saprò il tuo core,
recompense I will your heart,

adorarti ognor saprò.
adore you I always will.

FERRANDO, GUGLIELMO
Te lo credo, gioia bella,
I believe you, joy lovely,

ma la prova io far non vo'.
but the test I make don't want.
(I believe you, my beloved, but I won't put it to a test.)

DESPINA
Io non so se veglio o sogno:
I don't know if this is (a) dream:

Mi confondo, mi vergogno.

I'm confused, I'm ashamed.

Manco mal, se a me l'han fatta,

At least if I've been taken in,

ch'a molt'altri anch'io la fo.

that to many others I also take in.[30]

(At least if I've been taken in, I'll do the same to many others.)

TUTTI
ALL
Fortunato l'uom che prende

Fortunate the man who takes

ogni cosa pel buon verso,

every thing by the good side,

(Happy is the man who always looks on the bright side of things,)

e tra i casi e le vicende

and through the situations and the vicissitudes

da ragion guidar si fa.

by reason guide makes himself.

(lets himself be guided by reason.)

Quel che suole altrui far piangere

That which tends to others make weep

(What tends to make others weep)

fia per lui cagion di riso,

will be for him cause for laughter;

e del mondo in mezzo i turbini,
and in the world amid the whirlwinds
(and in the whirlwinds of the world)

bella calma troverà.
lovely calm he will find.

FINE DELL'OPERA
END OF THE OPERA

NOTES

Nico Castel

ACT I

1   *Ex cathedra*, literally "from a professor's chair."

2   *Ponno* is a poetic contraction of ***possono***, the present tense third person plural of *potere*, "to be able to," "can."

3   An Egyptian (Arabian, Indian, etc.) bird of fable, the only one of its kind, according to Greek legend said to live a certain number of years at the close of which it makes a nest of spices, sings a melodious dirge, flaps its wings to set fire to the pile, burns itself to ashes, and rises forth with new life. In Italian, the expression ***essere come l'araba fenice*** (to be like the Arabian phoenix) connotes "to be a unique thing, with no parallel." To the curious, it may be interesting to note that Metastasio defined it in his *Demetrio*, Act II, Scene 3: ***Come l'araba fenice, che vi sia ciascun lo dice, dove sia nessun lo sà***. Da Ponte was obviously acquainted with Metastasio's opus and grafted the phrase *verbatim* onto his libretto…

4   *Toccar con mano* (to touch with your hand), literally, **to give palpable proof.**

5   The **sequin** (*zecchino*) was a Venetian gold coin minted around the end of the 13th century, worth about $2.25 (from the Arabic *sikka*, *sekka*, a stamp, die).

6 Penelope, in Greek mythology, was the wife of Odysseus, noted for her fidelity.

7 It has already been pointed out in my Puccini and Verdi series that Italian words beginning with the letter **z** are variably pronounced by Italians. Despite the fact that the dictionaries (Zingarelli, Zanichelli, Melzi, Garzanti, etc.) specifically tell us that *zecchino* begins with a voiceless [ts] sound, it is a known fact that for centuries, Italians almost invariably have used a voiced [dz] sound on all words beginning with the letter **z**. Therefore, even though the correct was is [<u>ts</u>e´k:kino],one will almost always hear [<u>dz</u>e´k:kino]. The singer is cautioned to remain flexible on this point, especially if working with an Italian conductor or coach.

8 Cythera (or Khitira) is one of the Aegean islands. It is also the name given to Aphrodite, goddess of love, whose favorite island was Cythera.

9 An etymological tidbit for the curious: The Italian word *brindisi*, the Spanish *brindis* or *brindar*, or the French verb *brinder*, all meaning either "a toast" or "to toast," comes from middle age German, when the *Landesknechten* (Knights of the Land) used to offer each other drink and toasted each other by saying *Ich <u>bring dir's</u>* ("I'll bring it to you").

10 *Imeneo*, or its plural form *imenei*, is a poetic form for "marriage." *Nozze*, as in *Nozze di Figaro*, is a more common word. We will encounter *sposalizio* later on in *Don Giovanni*, and there is the ubiquitous *nodo* or its plural form *nodi*, meaning "knot," referring to the marriage knot. *Imene* is Hymen. Hymen, properly, is a marriage song of the ancient Greeks, later personified as the god of marriage, represented as a youth carrying a torch and a veil—a more mature Eros or Cupid.

11 This recitativo and Duettino No. 7 that follow are usually omitted in performance.

12 We have now seen **sword** referred to as *spada*, its common name, by the men in the opening scene, and now, within two sentences, by the girls, as *ferro* (iron) and *acciaro* (steel).

13 The organs of vision are normally called *occhi*. However, in libretti, one sees *pupille* (pupils), *rai* (rays), *lumi* (fires), and *ciglia/ciglio* (eyebrows/eyebrow).

14 Means of aquatic transportation have many names in poetic Italian. Here we see *barca* (ship/boat), *legno* (a small wooden boat). Then there is *naviglio, nave, vascelllo* (or its truncated form *vascel*). In Venetian tales, there is always the ubiquitous *gondola*.

15 *Diamine* is a mild expletive combining parts of two different words: *dia̲volo* (devil) and *Domi̲ne* (The Lord).

16 *Nascere* means many things in Italian: to be born, to come forth, to appear, to happen, to arise, to originate. One finds this poetic expression very often in libretti. The best translation is always, **what happened? what's up? what is it?**

17 The Eumenidies was the name the Greeks gave the Roman Furies. The Furies, according to mythology, were daughters of Night or of Earth and Darkness. They were three in number: Tisiphone (the Avenger of Blood), Alecto (the Implacable), and Megaera (the Jealous One). They were merciless goddesses of vengeance and punished all transgressors, especially those who neglected filial duty or claims of kinship, etc. Their punishments continued after death.

18 See note 2.

19 The best translation for this phrase is to use the colloquial expression **like murder**: "Make love like murder, as your lovers surely will on the battlefield."

20 *Per carità*, (literally "for charity's sake") and *Per pietà* ("for pity's sake") are interchangeable and mean the same.

21 *Rovesciare le macchine*, literally, "to upset the machinery," not unlike our "a wrench in the works." In this case the "machinery" refers to the intricate, complicated preparations, the detailed, painstakingly devised plot of Alfonso. We will encounter the same phrase about "upsetting the machinery" later on in this Mozart series in *Nozze di Figaro*, in Figaro's aria "Se vuol ballare."

22 An endearing diminutive for Despina, just as the boys called Don Alfonso *Don Alfonsetto* in the opening scene. Cherubino also calls Susanna *Susannetta* in *Nozze di Figaro*.

23 *Teco* is old Italian for *con te*, "with you." It comes from the Latin *tecum*. Two other similar words will be found in great abundance in the Mozart libretti and they are *meco*, for *con me*, "with me," and *seco*, for *con se*, "with him." In Catholicism the daily missal is called *vade mecum*, "it goes with me." In Spanish we have the modern remnants of this form in the words *conmigo*, "with me," *contigo*, "with you," and *consigo*, "with you" or "with himself."

24 *Giulebbe* comes from the Persian *gulap* meaning "sweet rose water," and by extension, anything sugary or very sweet. It's what the English word **julep** comes from (as in **mint julep**, that very sweet American Southern drink). For Despina, gold is the **sweetest thing** she can think of, and by extension…her **weakness**.

25 *Cacciare chiodo con chiodo* (to drive out one nail with another nail) is an Italian expression meaning to drive out one thought with another, a **love affair** with another (i.e., when a love affair is causing grief then it is replaced by another one.) It is said that the expression derives from an ancient Greek children's game, where a small wooden stick or metal rod was stuck in the soft earth and then driven out by another stick or rod thrown down to dislodge it.

26 **Wallachia**, or **Walachia** (In Italian it can be spelled *Valacchia* or *Vallacchia*, and its subjects *Valacchi* or *Vallacchi*), was a region in

Eastern Europe in what is now Romania and the Transylvanian region.

27 *Muso* is the word meaning the face of an animal, a snout, a muzzle, or in the case of humans, an ugly face, a mug, puss. A *muso duro* is a "sour puss."

28 The **accio/accia** suffix is a pejorative ending appended to Italian words. *Ragazza* is a girl, but *ragazza__ccia__* is a low-down, common gutter-snipe. *Donna* is a woman, but *donn__accia__* is a despicable, objectionable female.

29 We are talking here about poetic meter, not distance meter.

30 The word **_anime_** should have the stress on the first syllable. However, musically the stress falls on *an__i__me*, something that cannot be helped in this case, although in a recent hearing, an enterprising Fiordiligi changed the stress on that bar to make the word sound more like *__a__nime*.

31 *Fare una brutta (trista) figura* means "to look bad," as when someone makes you "look bad" (show your worst appearance).

32 A note for the studious and interested: The original Da Ponte libretto had several extra verses in the above aria, which Mozart never set to music:

Voi siete forieri di doci pensieri: chi guardavi un poco, di foco si fa.

You are harbingers of sweet thoughts: whoever looks at you, becomes enflamed.

Non è colpa nostra se voi ci abbruciate: Morir non ci fate in sì buona età.

It's not our fault if you enflame us. Don't make us die at such a young age.

33 These quotes refer to Ludovico Ariosto's (1475–1553) *Orlando Furioso*, (Canto XIX) in which Orlando's love for Angelica is challenged by Medoro, who suffers a serious wound in his chest at the hand of the Saracens.

34 Some texts read *son di bronzo i __suoi__ desiri* (__his__ desires are hard as bronze).

35   It is a known fact that both Da Ponte and Mozart were sensualists of one sort or another. Da Ponte's amorous escapades and ribald adventures are well catalogued, and one could tell from Mozart's salty letters to his friends and family that he wasn't above making occasional salacious references. This opera (and for that matter, all three Da Ponte libretti—including *Don Giovanni* and *Nozze di Figaro*) abounds with innuendo and puns with obvious sexual content. I will point these out to the reader as we go along, and refer them back to this "generic" note on the matter. The reader will have to use his/her imagination. Propriety per force restrains me from eludcidating too explicitly when these occasions occur.

36   Croesus ['kri:zʌs], the last king of Lydia (560–546 B.C.), was so rich and powerful that his name became proverbial for wealth. Many of the wise men of Greece were drawn to his court, incluing **Aesop**.

37   Narcissus, in Greek mythology, was a beautiful youth who saw his own reflection in the fountain, thought it was the nymph and jumped in trying to catch it and drowned.

38   Cyclops is one of a group or a race of giants. They had only one eye each, in the middle of the forehead, and their work was to forge iron for Vulcan.

39   Carlo le Pick (or Pich, or Picq), famous dancer and choreographer of the time, who danced in Mozart's ballet *Le Gelosie del Serraglio*.

40   See note 35.

41   *Porre il ditino in bocca*, is an expression meaning "to treat someone like a baby," alluding to a baby sucking his thumb.

42   A warning to the novice: in this case *color* (the truncated form of *coloro*) means "them." *Colore*, or its truncated form *color*, means "color."

43   The word *macchina* is the **verb** "to machinate," meaning to contrive a secret plan.

44   See note 35.

45   *Monsù* is a bastardization of the French *monsieur*. It is usually used in these libretti to address gentlemen of high rank or foreign origin.

46   For enterprising Despinas, a German accent is recommended. The salient characteristics of a German accent in Italian (or Latin) are as follows:

1. All initial **s** should be [z] *zalvete amabiles, ze molta, ze poca*.
2. All words having a [w] glide in it like ***dunque*** should be ***dun***kve. Also **kve***sto*.
3. All **r**'s should be gutteral [R].
4. All words with a [dʒ] cluster like (***cagione***) should be [katʃone] instead of [kaˊdʒone]. That goes for ***origine***, ***frigida***, ***coraggio***. The latter strongly pronounced as [kəˊRRat:tʃə].
5. To put the final stamp of German authenticity on the Italian, the occasional use of a [ə] schwa sound instead of the [e -ɛ] sound at the end of the words *forte*, ***cagione***, ***l'indole***, ***pozione***, ***affanate***, ***turbate***, ***celebre*** would be recommended.

47   The usual word in Italian for poison is *veleno*. However, *tossico* (or its contracted form *tosco*) is also used. It derives from the same root that give English the words **toxin**, **toxic**, **toxicity**, **toxicology**.

48   One finds ***bevvero*** and ***bebbero*** in different scores. It is the same meaning, just with a variant spelling.

49   She is referring to the famous (?) Anton Friedrich **Mesmer** (1734–1815), Austrian physician after whom **mesmerism** was named. He conducted experiments on the supposed curative powers of the magnet. He also developed the theory of animal magnetism, and conducted séances in Paris in which he purportedly cured a gamut of diseases. He was finally denounced as an imposter by the French government. In English, the words **mesmerize**, **mesmerizing**, **mesmerized** are derived from his name. He was also, incidentally, the owner of the property on which Mozart's *Singspiel Bastien und Bastienne* supposedly was performed for the first time.

50   The modern name for Germany in Italian is **Germania**. Here we find *Alemagna*, and in *Don Giovanni* we will encounter *Lamagna/Almagna*.

51   As is well known, the Spanish Conquistadores found immeasurable wealth in the New World, especially Mexico and Peru. Details abound telling of the Spaniards' cruelty, obsessed with transporting back to Mother Spain galleons brimming with gold booty pilfered from the native Americans. It's this Peru that eventually began to connote "weight in gold" in Italian.

52   *Pallas* is a stock epithet for the goddess Athena, commonly called Pallas Athena. Cythera is an island in the Aegean Sea, favorite spot of Aphrodite, Greek goddess of love (Venus), called *Citerea* in poetic Italian.

53   Despina should by now drop the German accent, once she is involved with other people or in the final ensemble.

ACT II

1   This is one of the rare instances in Italian when *gli* is pronounced [ɡli] and not [ʎi]: <u>negligere</u>, <u>negligenza</u> and <u>negligente</u>, meaning "neglect," "negligence," and "negligent." Also *glicerina* (glycerin), and *glìcine*, "wisteria."

2   Ganymede in Greek mythology was the cup-bearer of Zeus and a prototype of Greek male beauty.

3   A contraction of **possono**.

4   *Perchè* in Italian means both "why" and "because." The sense of "because" is being used here as an "excuse."

5   *Tenor* (a truncated form of *tenore*) means "the purport, the way, the manner," as when one says in English: "I don't like the **tenor** of your letter." The other meaning of *tenore* is, of course, the **tenor** voice, from the word *tenere* (to hold), indicating that the **tenor** "holds" the high vocal line in a chorus above basses and baritones.

6   Moreover, *pene*, pronounced [ˈpene], the word for "suffering, woe, misery, troubles," etc., is spelled the same as *pene*,

pronounced [`pɛnɛ], the male reproductive organ, the **penis**.
(This is one of the many pairs of **homographs** in Italian, words
spelled the same but pronounced with an open vowel instead of a
closed one (or vice versa), acquiring a totally different meaning.)
There is a possible intended salty pun here by the two conspira-
tors Da Ponte and Mozart. (See note 35 in Act I.)

7   And here comes the cause of the endless polemic. Is this a
misprint, or is it Italian of Da Ponte's time? The dictionaries
have no such verb as ***incoraggire***. They only show *incoraggiare*.
My esteemed colleague and supreme authority on *Così fan
tutte*, Renato Capecchi, an unimpeachable scholar on matters
Da Pontean, sustains that it is an old form of the modern verb,
yet all scores seem to have taken the matter into their modern
hands and "corrected" it to *incoraggiateli*. The final decision
must perforce rest with the conductor.

8   *Mongibello* is a curious Italian word of disparate etymologies
meaning "Mount Vesuvius," the volcano outside of Naples.
Half the word comes from the Latin *mons* (mountain), and
the Arabic *Jebel* (mountain). Of course, it contains *bello* in it
(meaning "lovely") and it is being applied to Dorabella's "fiery"
eyes. Let us not forget, however, that half the word derives
from *mons*, and that sends us right back…you guessed it…note
35 in Act I! (A geographic tidbit for those living in Colorado:
Outside Aspen, a few miles north, there is a little town called
El Jebel, very appropriately called "The Mountain.")

9   A basilisk is the king of serpents (from the Greek *basileos*,
"king"), also called a "cockatrice" and alleged to be hatched
from a cock's egg. It was reputed to be capable of "looking
anyone dead on whom it fixed its eyes." Also the name given
to a Central American lizard.

    The Basiliske…

From powerful eyes close venim doth convay
Into the lookers hart, and killeth farre away.
Spenser: *The Faerie Queene* IV, vii, 37.

10   *Tormi* is a contraction of *togliermi*. *Togliere* means "to take away," therefore *togliermi* (or *tormi*) means "take away <u>from me</u>."

11   *Ambo* and *terno* are lottery terms. If we apply it to New York horse racing terms, we could say that an *ambo* is a <u>daily double</u>, a *terno* is a <u>trifecta</u>, and a *cinquina* is a <u>quinella</u>. This most valuable information was supplied to me by one of the Metropolitan Opera's stagehands, Steve Diaz, an expert on matters of horse race betting.

12   Penelope was the faithful wife of Ulysses.

13   Mercury was the messenger of the gods.

14   *A quattro occhi*, literally "with four eyes," a variation of "eyeball to eyeball," except that in Italian it is "eyeballs to eyeballs," implying two people talking alone in confidence under a total of four eyes.

15   *Indorare* really means "to gild" (from *oro*, "gold"); *Indorare la pillola*, "to gild his pill," becomes "sweeten his pill" in English.

16   *Voler bene* in Italian means "to love," "to be fond of." The *vo'* is a contraction of *voglio*. Without the contraction, the line would be *Io voglio bene al sesso vostro*.

17   *Perchè* in Italian can mean "why?" and also "because." In English when one answers "because" one is giving **a reason** for something that has been asked. Therefore in this sense, *perchè* signifies "reason." Because of the repetition of the phrase *un gran perchè* at slower and faster tempi, it is a great help for the baritone to use assimilation in the faster passages to facilitate the delivery of this line, thus: [`an:nə `tʃɛrtə `uŋ `gra<u>m</u> per´ke]. In the slower tempo, the phonetic transcription above stands.

18   A saying that warns people not to boast about something before it is a certainty: "Don't count your chickens before they're hatched." With a similar ornithological bent, the Italians have the expression "don't sell the bird while it is still on the branch."

19   *Madamigella* is really "young lady," comparable to the French *mademoiselle*.

20 One also sees *settantamille* in some scores. It means the same, being a variant spelling of the other.

21 It's hard catching a handful of flies. The expression appropriately means empty-handed, and by extension, disappointed.

22 Artemis was an ancient Italian goddess, associated with Diana, the moon-goddess, also the goddess of hunting and the woodlands. Associated with fertility, she was worshipped by women.

> Queen and huntress, chaste and fair,
> Now the sun is laid to sleep.
> Seated in thy silver chair,
> State in wonted manner keep.
> Ben Johnson: *Hymn to Diana*

23 *In abrégé* is really French meaning "to shorten," "to cut short." Despina is referring to the curt (short) way in which Fiordiligi is giving her orders.

24 Perhaps this is a good time to say that the name *Fior –di –ligi* means "flower-of-devotion."

25 Charon in Greek mythology was the hideous old man who ferried the spirits of the dead across the river Styx in hell.

26 Vulcan was a son of Jupiter and god of fire. His workshop (grotto) was under Mount Aetna and other volcanoes, where he forged his metals.

27 In this case "octave" means a poem with eight stanzas.

28 In the 1996 production of *Così fan tutte* at the Metropolitan, that most charming of Italian singers Cecilia Bartoli opted to do the notary with a nasal voice as indicated, but added an outrageous American accent!

29 On the advice of that great scholar and colleague Renato Capecchi, I need to point out that we're dealing here with an "in-joke" by Da Ponte. It seems that ladies from Ferrara were considered to be not very virtuous and noted for their promiscuity. Albanian men were reputed to be well endowed sexually. So, it's back to note 35 in Act I...

30 *Farla a cualcuno* is an expression meaning "to do it to someone,"
    "to play a joke on someone," "to take someone in."